Harvard Shelter

How Two Small Southern California Cities Saved
Their Homeless Shelter

Kay Wilson-Bolton

MISSION
MATTERS
WE AMPLIFY STORIES

Mr. Century City, LLC

Managing Editor: Adam Torres / @AskAdamTorres

Editor: Hillary Crawford

Beverly Hills, CA 90212
www.MissionMatters.com

Paperback ISBN: 978-1-949680-57-7

Ebook ISBN: 978-1-949680-56-0

Many of the names have been changed, but the stories are true. Cover photo by: Zetong Li *on* Unsplash

CONTENTS

This book is dedicated to those who cry for people experiencing homelessness and actually do something.

- To Rudy Jiminez, the first brave man in Santa Paula who protected his homeless friends and unwittingly revealed their presence to our community. Until then, we didn't realize there were people in Santa Paula experiencing homelessness.

- To Howard Bolton (1933-2021), my faithful husband of 33 years, who never asked when I was coming home. And, who created dozens of posters, logos, signs, banners and all the graphics for the vehicles.

- To Tami Morford, my patient and loyal office manager. She did all the bookkeeping, grant reporting and accounting for 10 years without compensation, often on her own time, because there was no money to pay her.

- To Pastor Lupita Alonso, who died in July 2023. She was the faithful and energetic pastor of El Buen Pastor Methodist Church and Bardsdale Methodist Church. She hosted the first One Stop Operation in partnership with the County of Ventura Whole Person Care.

- To the colleagues who came alongside me over the years to do what they could to fill the gap.

- To the people who supported our work in so many ways, from day one.

- To every homeless person who believes there is no hope. There is. Don't give up.

The Truth:

"A candle is never brighter than when it is lighting another." —My version, adapted from the original statement by Thomas Jefferson and later the Rev. Timothy Keller. *"A candle loses nothing when it lights another candle."*

The Creed:

"Do all the good you can, by all the means you can, in all the ways you can, in all the places you can, at all the times you can, to all the people you can, as long as ever you can." —John Wesley, circa 1779

Acknowledgements

The main purpose of this book is to record a historic event, which occurred in Santa Paula California, a small town in Ventura County.

The story of Harvard Shelter is a story of passion and relentless commitment to do better, to Jesus' call to love God and love others. It began with the astonishing awareness that homelessness existed in my town. As I entered their world, I chose to love them and not label them. To do so is to libel them. Many people who joined our circle embraced this creed.

As the author, I invite you to learn, appreciate, ponder and help us resolve the issues we have been dealing with since 2008.

Other purposes of this book are to educate, enlighten and entertain. The stories of very real people in this book have various elements of tragedy, humor, loss and disappointment, failures and triumphs, hopes and fears. My hope is that after reading this book, everyone will be able to think kindly and speak softly of people who are experiencing homelessness or are in the line of fire to lose their shelter.

I lived each chapter of this book over a period of 15 years, from Christmas Eve morning 2008 to the present—September 2023. My writer and coach told me it was time to stop. I agreed to stop when I finally knew a two-year funding program was in place by the cities of Santa Paula and Fillmore, with funds matched by the County of Ventura, and a paid director was in place.

This heroic event is the result of the attention and dedication of Assemblymember Steve Bennett, of the 37th District in Ventura County. He made it his personal mission to craft and establish the two-year agreement with the help of his staff members, Atticus Reyes and Patricia Quiros.

This miraculous funding allows SPIRIT of Santa Paula to have enough money to hire a full-time paid executive director so I can step down. It provides more than $800,000 in annual funding to cover the monthly expenses and hire a second case manager and grant writer.

The real win is Harvard Shelter stays in business, sheltering and serving vulnerable people in the Santa Clara River Valley, who would otherwise be living in cars and other places not meant for habitation.

Other champions include Ventura County Supervisor, Kelly Long, of the 3rd District and her staff members Brian Miller and Manuel Minjares; Santa Paula City City Manager, Dan Singer; Santa Paula Community Development Director, Christy Ramirez; Finance Director, James Mason; Council members Jenny Crosswhite, Carlos Juarez, Andy Sobel, Pedro Chavez and Leslie Cornejo; and City Attorney Monica Castillo.

Also, Fillmore City Manager David Rowlands, all Council members involved in the support of Harvard Shelter, including Lynn Edmonds, Carrie Broggie, Christina Villasenor, Mark Austin, Albert Mendez and City Attorney Tiffany Israel.

Rosie Walker with the County of Ventura is the most patient instructor for HMIS (Homeless Management Information System.).

Since it is the role of the government to address the issue of homelessness, many vested people at the County of Ventura have helped us navigate our routes to ending it.

Some of our support comes from County CEO Sevet Johnson, Deputy CEO Mike Petit, Christy Madden, Tracy McAuley, Jennifer Harkey, Alicia Morales-McKinney, Morgan Saveliff, James Boyd and others.

Assemblymember Bennett and Senator Monique Limon were responsible for SPIRIT receiving a $1.5 million grant in October 2021 to improve the shelter and add 1,500 square feet of office space and classrooms. We call it the Launch Pad. While the building addition is extraordinary and took almost two years to complete, there was no funding for operations.

Special thanks to AIA Emeritus John Kulwiec and Interior Designer Susan Kulwiec. They are SPIRIT board members who were unwavering in their support and shepherded the complex construction project.

Other thanks to Kelly and Greg Ray, who just plain adopted us, beautified the building and edified everything they touched, especially with the personal visits from Santa Claus.

Thanks to our neighbors, the Fields family of Ventura Directional Drilling, and their employees, for giving us time to develop our expertise and beautify the building to match the beauty of theirs.

Thanks to Donohue Trucks for truck repairs along with Tarango Diesel Repair for monitoring the diesel trucks and thoughtfully rolling with the challenges of having so many homeless people in their driveway.

Thanks to Jeff Jacobs for volunteering his expertise as our amazing IT manager and fixing everything we could not.

Thanks to Pastors Adelita Garza, Robert and Liz Perez, and Father Charles Lueras, for bringing light into dark places and all the volunteers who help us do better.

Thanks to Cappi Patterson and her volunteers at Buddy Nation for helping us with the challenges of having homeless dogs, rather "dogs who are experiencing homelessness" and life with the people who are.

Thanks to Brent Reisender who believes it's his turn to pilot this ship. Start date was October 23, 2023.

Thanks to the people who served on the SPIRIT of Santa Paula board since its inception. You made a difference.

Board Members through the years from 2010-2023:

Howard Bolton, W. John Kulwiec, Bill Corrao, Susan Kulwiec, Dan McGranahan, Dr. William Simmons, Dawn Bavero, Dave Bavero, Teresa Villa, Veronica Sandez, Lupe Servin, Dana Tomarken, Jill Wallerstedt, Ned Branch, David Lippert, Jenny Arana, Jennie Cooksey, Mike Harrison, Lorissa Magdaleno, Bill Fowlie, Vern Alstot, Dan Goodwin, Betsy Chess and Norma Perez-Sandoval.

FOREWORD

BY STEVE BENNETT, CALIFORNIA ASSEMBLYMEMBER, 38TH DISTRICT

Kay Wilson-Bolton was selling real estate quite successfully in the Santa Clara River Valley when I met her in 2000, shortly after I was elected as a County Supervisor. Most of her clientele were not political supporters of mine. I assumed Kay was also on the other side of the divide. Even so, her pleasant, unassuming confidence was enough to keep our relationship cordial while we gradually got to know each other.

In 2008, Ventura County had been experiencing a strong rejection of homeless people for many years. City governments and individual citizens strongly resisted developing any homeless services. Just feeding the homeless became difficult. Building shelters, nearly impossible.

In the midst of all this, Kay Wilson-Bolton told me she was going to help the homeless population of Santa Paula. She had only recently become aware of their presence and need. I respected her sincerity, but was skeptical as to her ability to weather the personal attacks and rejection she would experience. A well-off white woman, with a business dependent upon the middle and upper classes of the Santa Clara River Valley leading this effort? No, not for long, I thought. How wrong I was.

Kay motivated a small, but dedicated group of volunteers, who each supplied their special talents. They persevered through 15 years of service to the homeless population in their community. It has changed them. More importantly, it has changed their community.

Kay's determination and tenacity earned her the respect of many skeptics. Readers of this book will appreciate how resistance to peer pressure and political hostility can be transformative for everyone. Those who endeavor to launch homeless shelter efforts in their community will gain immensely from this book. It provides a valuable inspirational message that is helpful during tough times. It also reveals key insights to the challenges that must be addressed for long-term success. This is particularly true when your shelter operates on a shoe-string budget and where separation of clients is so difficult.

We will never know how much faster and more effectively Kay and her team could have worked had they had access to this book when they launched their effort in 2008. This book will be invaluable for future efforts.

Kay shares her 15 years of insights with both warmth and toughness. She educated and inspired me. I believe readers of this book will be similarly moved.

The Giant of Homelessness

By Pastor Ron Urzua, First Presbyterian Church of Santa Paula

Thoughts on Fighting the Giant of Homelessness with the Power of Partnership

The Bible tells us about a teenager named David, who received courage and power from God to defeat a famous warrior and giant bully named Goliath with a slingshot. For the past 15 years, I have had the privilege of witnessing the power of partnership unleashed as a powerful force against the giants of homelessness, poverty and addiction in the city of Santa Paula, California. Yes, I'm a privileged witness! I have seen hundreds of church volunteers, churches of all denominations, community based nonprofits, business people, government officials and Santa Paulans of every stripe come together to collaboratively battle against the giant of homelessness in Santa Paula with love and action.

The powerful force of partnership, initiated and cultivated by the leadership of Kay Wilson-Bolton, has shown me that when several small groups come together, they can become a "giant" force for good causes. I suspect if certain cities are experiencing success in their local battles against the giants of poverty, homelessness and addiction, they are doing so through giant partnerships. Only giants can thwart giants.

The government will continue to work for solutions regarding homelessness, because doing so is a part of their responsibility. As a pastor, my concern is for the continued involvement of the larger church in the ministry to the poor and suffering. I often wonder what would happen if every single church in any given city participated in partnership in the battle against poverty, homelessness and addiction. To be sure, there are many churches in every city that are directly involved in faithfully serving the poor and the homeless. However, there are still too many churches not directly involved in ministry to the homeless. Having witnessed the power of partnership in Santa Paula, I'm convinced if the vast majority of churches, synagogues, temples, para ministries and various faith groups ever began to partner with each other in ministry, they would become a giant and mighty force in the battle against homelessness.

Therefore, it is of vital importance that both pastors and faith leaders regularly remind their congregants that in addition to feeding people the Word of God, we must also feed them with food when necessary. Christ's two miracles of multiplying small amounts of bread and fish to feed a crowd of 4,000 and later a crowd of 5,000 demonstrates that Jesus thought it was important to give bread to the hungry. Yes, He gave people the Word of God, but He also thought providing "bread" was important.

If Jesus thought the ministry of providing people with bread was important, His Church must also take the ministry of providing bread seriously. The church must avoid the widespread false dichotomy that says the church should only focus on feeding people with God's Word so it is not distracted by social causes and meeting people's felt needs. The church is called to both the ministry of the Word and to the ministry of "bread." As individual churches, we must also care about "bread" like Jesus did and form partnerships with one another, in order to become God's local giant solution to the problems of poverty, homelessness and addiction in every city.

INTRODUCTION

This book is written to and for those of us who have become numb to the misery of people living their life under the label of "homeless." I don't use more polite words like "unsheltered" or "unhoused." Any lesser name is a distraction from the dark side of being homeless.

Please remember that homeless is a noun. It's a thing. Homeless is not an adjective that describes someone. This is a favorite reminder of Christy Madden in the CEO's office for the County of Ventura. Someone may be homeless. They are not a homeless "someone." I will try to refer to his part of our communities as people who are experiencing homelessness.

My mission is to educate and inform, while providing a close-up view of the heart and soul of dedicated volunteers and underpaid staff who believe in the dignity of every person and the value of second chances ... and third, and fourth and fifth.

Some of the stories are funny, because the events described cannot be manufactured. Consider the 75-year-old mother (with a PhD in music interpretation and composition) and her 50-year-old son with a chronic illness living at Harvard Shelter.

They convinced us the only specialist in the field of William's rare auto-immune disease is at the medical center two hours away in Irvine, California. They convinced another Harvard Shelter guest, Stephen, into driving them to Irvine and telling him they would pay for his motel if he would drive and bring them home the next day after the treatment.

As they neared Irvine, they told Stephen to keep driving, because they learned the physician was in St. George, Utah. Stephen was driving their car with expired tags and became very nervous. But he continued on.

When they arrived near their destination, it was nighttime and cold. They called me and asked for money for the motel ... $200. We did not know where they were until she gave the Western Union address in Utah. No Zelle, no Venmo. Our case manager found a Western Union site and wired money for the motel.

Police pulled them over outside of St. George for expired tags. Stephen sat outside in the cold for an hour while police tried to decide what to do. They knew towing the car would create an extreme hardship. Stephen got a ticket for driving a car with expired tags, even though it wasn't his car.

William received his treatment. They spent the night together in the motel and had breakfast. With the last bit of money, they put gas in the car and arrived back at the shelter.

William was feeling fine, but Stephen was mad and a wreck over his apparent hijacking. Mom was convinced Stephen had a great time and they look forward to traveling with him again soon.

While there are occasional moments of levity, the majority of our encounters range from heartbreaking to anger-inducing to downright scary. One of the biggest issues facing Santa Paula, and every other community, is the lack of affordable housing. It's pricey in Ventura County, due to our proximity to the coast and our weather is so moderate. But the people who work in the service industries, like gas stations, restaurants and hotels, have to drive 50 miles to find an affordable place to rent. We are working on an initiative to require communities to provide housing for the people who work there.

There are many good reasons to do that. However, the luxury communities of the world don't agree. They want to be around people like them. They want and need people to show up for work, but they don't want them to live near them.

If a pack of homeless poodles was living in the riverbed, there would be a mass effort to rescue them. But because they are homeless *people*, they are largely shunned, ignored, despised, rejected and bypassed. Poodles would never be bypassed. Homeless people are a different story. Consider Maggie.

One warm spring morning in Santa Paula, Maggie was seen at the corner of our gateway intersections with two shopping carts, sofa cushions, luggage with wheels, bags of food, a watermelon and what any reasonable person would call a variety of trash.

I decided to intercept her before someone posted a picture on Facebook declaring death to homeless people.

Maggie knows I'm gentle with her so she was willing to strike up a conversation about all her treasures and the food she had collected at local food pantries over the last couple of days.

I asked her if she would be interested in an interview for our Bruised Reeds podcast. She said I could record her voice, but not her face. Due to a car accident many years ago, she has an ugly scar above her right eyebrow that distorts her features. I asked if she was connected to Behavioral Health and she admitted, "Sometimes." She went on to say, "I know I'm ugly and a problem for people, and I'm confused by the voices."

I needed to address the mess she had created before complaints from the public and the restaurant owner began, but I decided to chat first about her plans for the day. She stated she needed to get to Piru so she could wash clothes and get cigarettes. Piru is a neighborhood in the county, rural and with few services. I asked how she planned to get there. She wasn't sure, because the voices in her head were confusing her, but cigarettes help her ignore them.

Gentle conversations are necessary so our street people don't hear us sounding like law enforcement. I asked if I could pray for her, asking God to silence the voices so she could only hear One, the Right One. She started to cry and let me touch her shoulder as I did that.

As I pondered how to address her moving from this spot, I could tell traffic was beginning to slow and gawk. To make or maintain a relationship with someone like Maggie, it is important to speak differently than law enforcement does. Their typical conversation includes, "You can't do that," "You can't stay here" and "You are making a mess." When I asked about when she planned to move, she stated she wasn't sure, because she was bothered by all the voices, reminding her of all her bad decisions. Thankfully, some officers are beginning to adapt their practices to include "Trauma Informed Care."

I told her people were going to start complaining to the police about her treasures. She responded, "Everyone better stay out of it. There are too many people involved. When my mom used to make tamales she would always tell us there were too many hands in the masa. I feel like there are too many hands in my masa today." Maggie has no control over the voices and does not see herself ever living in what we call normal circumstances. She has a husband and children in a nearby city. She thinks he has a girlfriend.

I helped her organize her stuff and move it off the sidewalk in the shade of the local restaurant where she slept that night. I spoke to the restaurant owner, assuring her she would be on her way.

Later in the day, Maggie was still in the same spot. She had tidied up a bit and was sitting in the shade.

Who will rescue Maggie?

Let's face it. If Maggie was a poodle, there would be a race to see who could get there first. She isn't. However, she is someone's daughter, sister, and mother of three boys. Since she isn't a poodle, the only race is by the posse who wants her "outta here."

She is despised by many. Abandoned by all. Feared by others.

Maggie is not afraid of me, because I am gentle and speak to her kindly—except for the day when I thought she kidnapped my cat from my real estate office. That's another story.

The next day was Sunday, and I saw her a block away from Saturday's outpost with her sofa cushions piled on top of her cart. She used them for her bed behind the shrubs near the restaurant. I'm sure she didn't make it to Piru, and I wondered if she got any cigarettes.

Such things are always on my mind. Aren't we compelled to love people more than poodles? Yes, we are, and we can love both. I will rescue a poodle any day, but not before I hold out my hand to a lonely woman living on the streets of my community, hearing voices that are telling her she isn't good enough to live in a safe place.

The SPIRIT of Santa Paula and the Harvard Shelter are committed to preventing and ending homelessness in the Santa Clara River Valley. We are also committed to serving the least powerful among us with food, services, encouraging words, direction, resources and compassion.

My personal goal is to be the warm fire that people are drawn to.

*"Maggie" — a Santa
Paula traveler.*

*These adorable pups were born at the Shelter
and adopted immediately—makes my point
about poodles.*

Part One

Birth of a Mission

Mr. Century City, LLC

Chapter One

SHOCKING REALIZATIONS

The winter of 2008 was cold, and the global economy was unraveling. On Christmas Eve morning, I took a different route to meet my husband at a local restaurant for an early breakfast. I noticed a fire engine and the medical examiner's vehicle in the parking lot of a local church and stopped to see if I could help. The fire captain said they were getting ready to ask for a Chaplain and my timing was perfect. I am the Lead Fire Chaplain for the Ventura County Fire Department. He continued, "We had a homeless guy die in the church last night. The janitor is really upset."

When I went to console the janitor, there sat my friend, Rudy Jimenez, who has his own problems, but a heart of gold. The church hired him as a janitor, and he admitted to letting a dozen or so homeless people into the church at night, because it was so cold that year. The man who died was Richard Rios Soto. I learned Richard was 38 years old and lived in Santa Paula. I wondered how it could be that he was not at home, with family or in the hospital.

The medical examiner told me Richard was going to die that night. "Lucky for him, he died in a church." The pastor of the church saw nothing good and only the potential danger of Rudy's actions, so Rudy was fired with no discussion about what the church could do to help. Rudy never dreamed this would happen. He had nothing to do with Richard's death. He put his friends first. He was the brave one who risked his own security and got fired, but he saved close to a dozen lives in the process.

In a flash, it dawned on me that we had homeless people in our town. I didn't know that. I lived the kind of life that I didn't have to know. As it turned out, hardly anyone in Santa Paula knew we had homeless people. I decided right then to do something.

That began my journey into an unknown and daunting world of homelessness. Little did I know, God had been packing my bag for this assignment and shaping my life for this work for some time.

A Journey of Faith

My first memory of having a tender heart on this subject was around the age of four, when I watched the hobos (the old name for transients) sit at the stoop outside our back door, eating a plate of beans and hot dogs, homemade bread, butter and blueberry jam offered by my mother. There must have been a secret sign somewhere directing them to the Gibersons on the Old Dover Road in Gonic, New Hampshire. They were not allowed inside, but mom never turned them away.

Back in 2002, I was one of eight people—Bill and Linda Simmons, me and Howard Bolton, and Bill Corrao and his wife—who gathered in the home of John and Susan Kulwiec, where we decided to organize ourselves around the concept of "doing something good" for the community. Six years later, on Christmas Eve morning, we found our purpose.

On Christmas Day—the day after Richard died in the church—Sgt. Jimmy Fogata led me and my friend, Cathy Schneir, into the riverbed where we could see and meet homeless people. I was shocked and fascinated at the same time. I met people that day who became friends.

The day after Christmas 2008, I called on Kate Mills, Director of Ventura County Public Health Clinic and One Stop; Carol Schulkin, Director of Homeless Services; and Cathy Brudnicki, charged with completing the County's 10-year plan to end homelessness. My pastor, David McKeever, also joined us.

My plan was to open a shelter immediately, but I learned there are many obstacles to doing that—location, manpower, supplies and permits (yes, permits). We agreed to plan for a shelter and begin a hot meal program.

The Miracle of Many Meals

Somewhere in my past, I learned if you can't have someone stay in your home for safe sleep, the next best thing is to feed them. That played out on January 14, 2009. It was the early days of email and I remember sending 25 people an email asking for help. I suggested they prepare a dish for their family and an extra one for us.

When Jesus said, "Feed my sheep," we took that literally. Pope John Paul II said, "Pray for people who are hungry. And then feed them."

The hot meal program, aptly named *Many Meals,* started in a local church, Iglesia de Dio 7mo Dia at 208 South Mill Street. The kitchen was minimal, only two burners on the stove worked and the oven only heated to a low level. It was a challenge to set up and clean.

Back then, I didn't know anyone who was homeless and I wasn't sure how to convince them to come for dinner. So, we placed flyers in well-traveled places like certain corner grocery stores, paths to and from the river, and the County's Resource Center on Main Street for everyone to see.

January 14, 2009, was a Wednesday. We chose mid-week, thinking we would fill the gap. We spent the next 14 years trying to fill gaps.

That first meal was two weeks after Richard died and it was unknown if anyone would come. I remember that foggy January night as I waited at the window to see if anyone would show up. I wondered who they would be and I'm sure they wondered the same about me. I will never forget the thrill of watching them walk toward us. We were prepared for 30 people and 47 people came. We ate family-style and became acquainted. As we broke bread together over the next few weeks, we became like family. Some of those relationships still exist today, except for those who have died. It was about trust for them. It was about giving hope for me. It wasn't long before our numbers were in the 60s and we served in shifts.

This is our first Many Meals on January 14, 2009.
We served in shifts, because the space was so limited.
Some of the guests are deceased.
Homelessness takes a heavy toll.

Cathy Brudnicki was the Chairman of the County's 10-year Task Force to End Homelessness. I remember asking how many people she thought we could serve each week and she guessed it could go as high as 200. That number quickly turned into 600 meals a week.

Within a year, I approached Ronnie Urzua, my pastor at First Presbyterian Church, about moving Many Meals to their fellowship hall and spacious kitchen. I had been a member there since about 1976 and I thought that would buy me some goodwill and support. I suggested writing a letter to the session, and he said, "Let me handle it." I knew why.

It was not a popular idea with many in the church. The congregation consisted of what would be considered the old white guard of Santa Paula and their view of welcoming Mexican people into the environment was not as welcoming as I had hoped. One member suggested the Mexican kids would probably put cookies in their pockets. They probably did.

It was a rough go for many months. Some weren't happy about having "those people" in the building. But as time went on, they began to talk to our dinner guests and know them as mothers and grandmothers. The leadership of the church eventually came to see the faces of people enjoying the surroundings as people who were children and had children suffering from economic challenges. Many Meals became their ministry, too, and it evolved into *Church at the Park*, in order to reach those not inclined to come to church.

There was a time when there wasn't enough money to buy cheese or utensils for that week's meal. I relied on donations wherever I could get them. In fact, I was having financial challenges of my own during those years of global economic meltdown.

I would visit Food Share on Wednesday mornings to see what was available and hoped it wasn't frozen. I would gather what I could from any location and buy only necessities at local grocery stores. I could count on Tresierras to have Roma tomatoes at 29 cents a pound. Today, they are $1.29 a pound. I was usually frantic by noon and frazzled as I met the cooks to talk about the recipes. Mainstays were trays of orange

slices for beauty and garnish, salad or coleslaw, mashed
potatoes, and rice donated faithfully each week by El Pescador
Restaurant—always for 600 people. Occasionally their cook would
forget the rice and we would have disaster.

Garman's Pub supplied the beautiful bags of fresh carrots each week
so we could count on a fresh vegetable.

Emily Cantero would start the cooked beans on the stove at 10 a.m.,
during the Women to Women Bible Study group. We always had a
hot dish such as lasagna, chili beans or Shepherd's pie. I'd have to
get creative with menus once I knew the available ingredients.

There was a core group of cooks who became my weekly emotional
support group and right arm. They began to count on each other
to take on various tasks, such as washing and sanitizing the trays,
slicing and prepping this and that and crafting the food into beautiful
presentations. One or two would stay until the food was hot and
monitor the temperature until the serving volunteers, supervised
by Bill Fowlie and Micah Chapman, arrived at 4 p.m. to butter the
carrots, dress the coleslaw and heat the trays to 165 degrees for 17
seconds one last time. A separate group of volunteers arrived around
2 p.m. to set up the food pantry for take-home food supplies.

Another crew volunteered to wash dishes, a difficult task before we
discovered pan liners. The cooks were Melinda and Marty Pettit,
Sue and Ian McAlister, Gary Pangelina from Camarillo, Steve and
Cathy Goch, Carol Elliott, Monty Clark, Bob Roberts, Ken Ary, Jerry
Gibbs, Little Kathy Wilbur and Andrea Worthen, who suffered from
Anorexia. Andrea was brave because it was hard to be around food.
More volunteers would arrive for cleanup. Thanksgiving and Christmas
dinners were never missed, even if the Wednesday fell on the holiday.
We never missed a meal. We realized it wasn't just homeless people who

were hungry, but also people struggling to provide food for themselves and their families.

While the weekly numbers grew to about 600, our record was one Thanksgiving dinner when the number exceeded 1,100. That year, students from the Master's University helped serve the meal. They were accompanied by Dr. Ernie and Rose Baker from the Biblical Counseling Department—my professor, too. One student serenaded the dinner guests with his violin.

Wednesdays became family night out for many. They sat at round tables, communed and commiserated. There were a number of single dads who brought their kids, even estranged couples would meet for a get-together. It seemed like a miracle every week, until week number 571.

I'll always remember the Wednesday of the week COVID-19 was announced as a pandemic. The church manager, Chris Buchanan, and I stood in the kitchen, looking into the dining room, and I commented, "You know, we're going to have to shut this down." And, that's what we did. I knew it was more important than ever that the food supply continue, so we switched to a food pantry. As it turns out, due to a Food Rescue program, and as a partner of CalRecycle and Ventura County Public Health, we were able to gather food bags worth at least $100 and generally 25 to 50 pounds each week. We often provided more than people could carry and so they began bringing carts and baby carriages. We've been able to serve more people with more food. Once again, God took a bad situation and made it great. Our visitors receive far more food and many more are served.

How One Thing Leads to Another

A necessary and welcome event in the life of someone on the streets is a hot shower and clean clothes. Without a shower and someone to monitor the activity in a central location, this remains a dream. In the spring of 2016, there was a leadership conference at the Reagan Library for high school students. Iriz Perez was a senior that year and came home inspired by former council member Laura Espinosa to do something great. Iris presented a plan to me to provide just that—hot showers and clean clothes.

We took the idea to a broader audience and caught the attention of the Public Health Department and the Continuum of Care, who agreed to purchase three shower pods from a company call CarePodz, owned by George Magana and retired Ventura County Fire Chief, Vern Alstot, who later became a SPIRIT board member. The decision was unanimous to assign one of the pods to Santa Paula. The location was at El Buen Pastor United Methodist Church, which was the forerunner of the One Stop service model to connect people to services, including medical care. That program still exists today and is sponsored by the County of Ventura, Human Services Agency. Iris Perez went on to be a successful Realtor in Ventura County and is still inspiring people to do better.

Shelter Beginnings

The first year of seasonal shelter was held in 2009 at the same church on South Mill Street. There were 15 to 20 guests each night. We slept on the hard floor, coughed and laughed. I was there four or five nights a week. Volunteers stepped up to relieve me. My husband was sick at the time and was facing a leg amputation, but he never said, "When are you coming home?" I was working on my master's degree at the time at the Master's University, and was struggling with my responsibilities as well as my full-time job as a real estate broker. I ran several Century 21 offices at the time and was struggling to keep everything moving forward.

What I didn't see coming was God stripping everything from me, shaping and battering me for His work. In 2009, it was apparent I could move through the chairs of the California Association of Realtors to State President. The night the traveling team was in Sacramento, a close friend and I were both nominated for the office that would move me forward. Had Stuart Monteith not been nominated, I would have been happy. But, because she had been, my heart was not in for a campaign. I let the others go to dinner and I went to my room. Trying to sleep, I heard the still small voice of God say, "Kay, I want you to come with me. I have something for you to do."

I did and He certainly did.

Compassion Under Fire

I did not anticipate the hostility that would come from people who had been my friends. An early supporter was the minister of the Unitarian Universalist Church, Carolyn Price. I've learned over the years that only the kindest of hearts will help and not hinder, encourage and not criticize, support and not tear down.

As our support for our homeless people emerged, so did the objections. In 2010, a new city manager arrived. His name was Jaime Fontes, and he told the community he would be unlike our very popular and affable Wally Bobkiewicz, who left Santa Paula for Evanston, Illinois. He also said he would lead from the background.

Those in the business community who opposed us had his ear early on and the tension began to rise. A mediation and roundtable meeting was called at the Unitarian Universalist Church. It was ugly. People who had been my friends glared at me from across the room, particularly a local business owner. I thought I was in another world. Community leaders decided I was a bad person and was single-handedly ruining the economy of the city. No progress was made at the meeting. Everyone became firmly entrenched in their positions, including me.

As tension mounted, Unitarian Universalist Church minister Carolyn Price asked the new city manager for a meeting to talk about the homeless problem and possibilities. It was mostly to defend ourselves and to ask for some support. We asked for one hour. Jaime Fontes started the meeting and for 25 minutes, he talked about himself. I interrupted him and told him we did not come to talk about him, but instead the problems in the community regarding homeless people. The meeting was non-productive and each of us left frustrated and confused about next steps.

My real estate office was located in a prime commercial area with a private entrance at the rear. As we started to serve simple breakfasts at the back door to street folks, two neighbors began to complain about what they thought was me single-handedly growing the homeless population.

Jaime Fontes called a meeting at city hall. He said I could bring two supporters and the woman complaining could bring two. She brought the directors of two museums, I brought two pastors, Don Loomer and Ronnie Urzua. The tone was incredibly hostile. Mr. Fontes turned to me and asked me to start the meeting. I told him I did not call the meeting, and anyone else could speak. It was brutal. The hate from someone who has no experience with poverty, drug addiction or hunger was on the attack. The rest of the meeting is a blur.

My resolve hardened. I was never insensitive to the impact of homeless people in public places. They make a mess. They have bad habits. Those with substance abuse issues steal anything they can, and their appearances are offensive to those without sympathy.

I call them "my people," because any other words are painful and mischaracterize the person. As more of my people knew they could get coffee and food in the early morning and started to gather, the nearby businesses began to express concern. I was always torn between my desire to be a good neighbor to those around me and my obligation to care for others.

As God does things, I decided to sell the building. It went for a handsome price to Lee Cole, president of Calavo, Inc.. He had purchased the historic building next door and donated it to the local Art Museum. He eventually donated my building to the same organization to be used as an art center in honor of his wife, Jeanette Cole.

In the summer of 2015, a client called and asked me to show him a commercial building at 113 N. Mill Street, a block away in a less-traveled alley. When his offer was not accepted, I left a note inside the building stating to "whomever the new owner might be" that I wanted to be his new renter. Within a few days, Brian Bresolin from Santa Barbara called and asked when I wanted to move in. Had my client purchased the building, that new location would not have been mine.

The building had 1,500 square feet at the front for my real estate business and 1,500 square feet at the rear for homeless services, a kitchen, two bathrooms and a two-car enclosed garage we used for our food pantry. It was perfect. Maria Sanchez and Maria Artelejo were hostesses preparing meals and sharing information about services. Maria Sanchez was close with many of our guests and would forget we had rules about when they could visit. She was known for staying late in the evening to serve food and keep people warm. We knew it couldn't last long, because neighbors knew the travelers and their drug habits.

We were there for five years until God opened the floodgates and introduced us to Naomi Pitcairn, who played an important role in the evolution of SPIRIT of Santa Paula by donating the building that became Harvard Shelter.

We are always amazed at the number of people who wish us well and provide financial support to keep us doing what we love and have learned well. We are especially grateful to our attorney, Ben Schuck, for his shepherding in the early days, by preparing the corporate documents. He and Katherine Becker continue to advise us on the various issues businesses encounter.

Chapter Two

BLESSINGS AND HUMBLE BEGINNINGS

In 2010, Wells Fargo Bank donated a house to SPIRIT of Santa Paula. It had been foreclosed on and was an environmental disaster. They could not sell it and were willing to donate it to a nonprofit. As evidence of another amazing connection, the listing broker was a friend, Fritz Kling. He called one day to ask if we wanted the house. Our board thought it would be a good use for a homeless shelter for up to six people. Rod Elliott owns the local land moving and commercial water line installation company, and he knew exactly what the county needed us to do to remove the environmental citations.

The remediation cost was $80,000. We promised to pay him back when the house was sold, and we did.

Once the home was in good condition, we were able to open quickly. It was a self-policing living situation and turned out to be far more difficult than we thought, even though we were warned it would be. Addicts were far more clever than I was back then, and they were able to continue living their secret lives. The neighbors were not happy with us, especially with me, and I understand why. We are lucky nothing serious happened. We decided to sell the house after two years. It was too far from town and services. Discipline was difficult.

Against my better judgment, a police officer encouraged me to have an open house for neighbors to meet us prior to opening. That was not a good idea. The neighbor threatened me and raised his hand, but a board member stepped in. I later learned the neighbor was the father-in-law of the police officer who suggested the open house.

We had three more years of winter shelter at the El Buen Pastor Church, overseen by a welcoming, but wary group of trustees. Since drug use is at the heart of most homelessness, we had our share of misbehaving. The trustees were struggling with our presence and God's call on them to be open to serving the community. We closed the shelter for three years.

One rainy season in 2017, we were called on by the city manager and fire chief, Rick Araiza, to manage the emergency shelter at the Community Center. I always wondered why a shelter was viewed as valuable in an emergency, but not in very cold weather.

Relationships continued to change. My friends moved away from me. No one invited us to parties anymore. Our circle became very small, but God was always at the center. I had new friends.

In 2018, the longtime, supportive First United Methodist Church with the beautiful fellowship hall and semi-commercial kitchen, closed its doors. I contacted the church district office and asked if we could open a winter shelter there. They were quick to say "yes." By then, we had a new city manager named Michael Rock. He was in complete opposition to the opening of a shelter, due to the harsh reactions coming from area businesses, especially the historic hotel across the street. The hotel owner warned Rock if he allowed us to open, she would sell the hotel to a drug rehab clinic. We learned later the owner was already in negotiations with a Westlake service provider to do just that.

It was raining that winter and we set up the shelter so we could be ready to open. Michael Rock threatened me to not open. He was on vacation and would not be back until after Jan. 1. He made us wait, even though trusted staff could have handled the paperwork. When he returned, I invited him to the site so he could see how clean the hall was and how organized we were.

He also learned some of Santa Paula's leading business owners, David and Tracy Lippert, donated $10,000 for us to operate the shelter. That was a turning point. He softened and approved the temporary permit to operate. Tracy and David were God's instruments in that effort. They still are.

One particular rainy night in January 2019, Pastor Adelita Garza escorted 17-year old shelter guest, Vannity Alonso, to a city council meeting. They both addressed the council, thanking them for allowing the shelter to be opened. Pastor Adelita noted the gesture represented the personality of a kind and generous community.

Vannity spoke eloquently about her mother and little brother, stating they would be homeless somewhere if he had not allowed the shelter to open. Shelter guests watched their presentation on TV and everyone was moved. At that time, the impression of homeless people was anything but children and their single parent. Michael Rock told me later, after he left Santa Paula, he was emotional during their comments. Reality checks can do that.

We housed at least 10 children, single mothers and senior citizens that winter. In that group were Nomi Marrufo and Sabriana Marrufo. They went on to become employees of SPIRIT of Santa Paula and are worthy of their own chapter in this book. There were at least 60 guests that season. Despite the continuing cold weather, Michael Rock made us close on March 1, 2019.

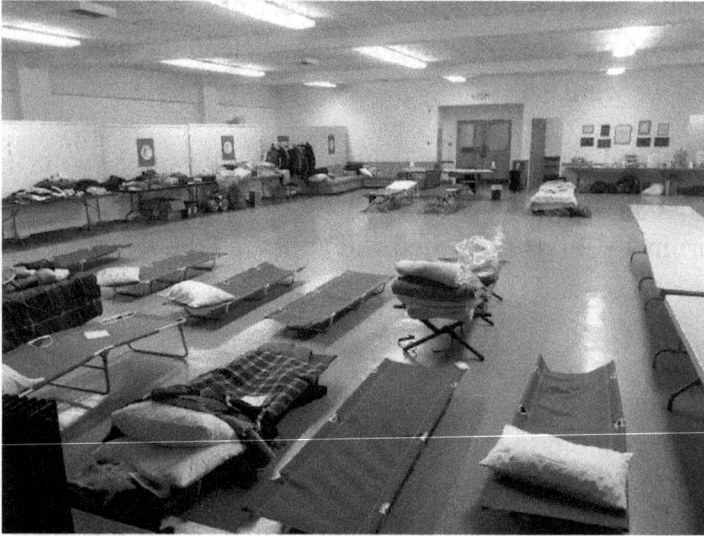

Wesley Hall is the site of the 2018-2019 winter shelter. There were no showers and only two bathrooms. At least it was warm, and we can never thank the First United Methodist Church enough for allowing Wesley Hall to be utilized.

Our Current Shelter Location

Sometime in 2018, during a Saturday morning breakfast at the Santa Paula Airport Café, my husband Howard and I began a conversation with Naomi Pitcairn, a newcomer to town. I learned she had been a wall dog, painting the sides of tall buildings in New York. Such coincidences are actually miracles. My husband, Howard Bolton, had been a wall dog in Los Angeles, painting the sides of theaters for upcoming attractions.

Naomi was born a woman of privilege, yet had a heart for every lost person. She was an artist, a political activist, and as it turned out, a lover of homeless people, having worked on the streets of the Bay area. She became a cheerleader for our organization and our work.

Our friendship evolved over time and one day she suggested I find her an investment property. Susan Kulwiec, a SPIRIT board member, found a well-known building in foreclosure and bankruptcy online. I suggested the building to Naomi and she acted quickly. The asset manager only gave us 10 days for inspections, but we completed tests for mold, asbestos, termites, sewer, roof, electrical and plumbing.

We learned the building had a fire in about 2015 and in order to reopen, the owners were required to install sprinklers, a new roof, new heating and air conditioning, electrical and handicap bathrooms. This resulted in extra value for the property and unbelievable savings moving forward.

I asked Naomi to consider leasing us the building for a shelter. She agreed and said the terms would be no rent for 30 years.

The building was an old bar on Harvard Boulevard, known over time as Buck and Sonny's, the Frontier Club and El Gramo de Oro. Since the building was away from town, the potential for objections decreased. When locals realize where the shelter is located, it gets a laugh or two.

As God does things, our board consisted of a Realtor, an architect and an interior designer—all the talent in one room to work for acquisition, design, construction and occupancy. We dedicated our building on a rainy Friday, Dec. 6, 2019, and opened for our first night the following day—the same day I had to move my office to the new Mill Street location. It rained and rained.

We did our best to redesign the old bar that became the SPIRIT of Santa Paula's Harvard Shelter, to make it look like a commercial building along Harvard Boulevard. If you drove by, you would not know it was a homeless shelter. The wide double doors open into a large area that looks like a gymnasium. It's not that big, but wide open. To the right is the old stage. We originally put the women and children up there, but they were so messy that we moved them down so we could monitor them. Then, we put the men who work up there, because they come and go at all hours. That was worse, so we are back to women and children. Yes, it's still messy.

This is the Harvard Shelter building as it was when we envisioned it being a safe place for families, seniors and adults with life's greatest challenges. It had a sketchy history known as Buck and Sunny's Bar, the Frontier Club, and El Gramo de Oro. The visionary was Naomi Pitcairn who purchased the building and then deeded it to SPIRIT for use as a shelter.

With the new construction and design, there is a male and female bathroom and a large shower at the south end. We had to install a pump to take the sewage up to the street level. I hope that things work forever. Off to the left of the big double doors, is our commercial kitchen area. We put tables up and take them down after meals so they're not taking up space all day. Beyond that are offices and our food storage room with refrigerators and freezers. Beyond that are two handicap bathrooms and a handicap shower. At the end of the hallway is where we have a new addition, which houses a classroom, two offices for administration, reception, staff restroom, laundry facility and a kitchen area for staff.

Harvard Shelter in Fall of 2023. The original cost was $550,000 and it has since been improved by over $1.5 million thanks to grants and donors. The new addition was dedicated on August 24, 2023.

The shelter is congregate living, meaning there's one big room with bunk beds. We try to put the men on one side and women on the other side with—forgive me—with the least enticing females in the middle so there's a separation. They pass each other in the hallway on the way to the bathrooms.

When the shelter opened, I knew I had to be careful with food preparation, and my cook couldn't work seven days a week. Laura had been a chef in her home country of El Salvador and was staying at Harvard Shelter. She volunteered for a while, but I realized she deserved to be paid. Thanks to the case management of Jessica Lucas, Laura got her green card, her California ID and Social Security card, which made her eligible to work and be paid legally.

Since employment laws were in place, we wanted to honor them and her. So, I went back to the Many Meals crew and asked if they would be willing to pick up the task and meet on Friday morning to prepare seven trays of food for Harvard Shelter's weekend and street outreach. This would provide food for the weekends and all staff has to do is put it in the oven and bring it to the proper temperature.

I have my Kitchen Manager Certificate and everyone who works in the kitchen has their food safety certificate.

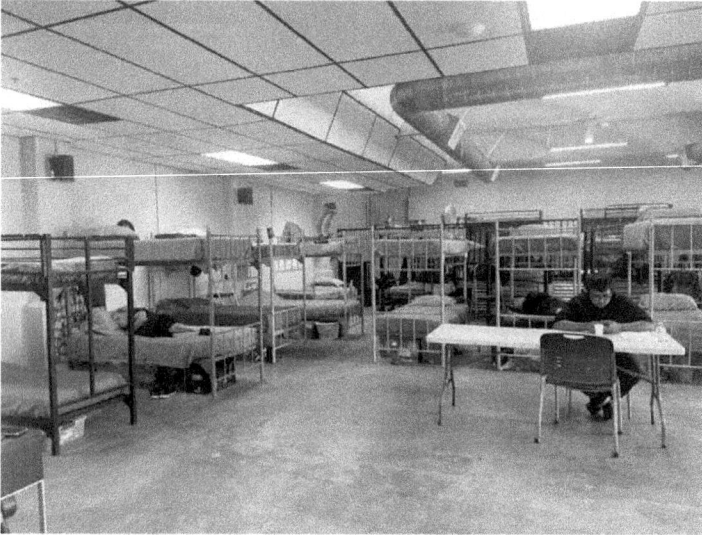

The new bunk beds show the new space in Harvard Shelter. There are now four bathrooms and three showers. The warming kitchen allows us to serve 75 meals a day to guests and visitors at the Drop In Center.

We were used to commercial kitchens, because Bernadine McCracken, a longtime member of the Presbyterian Church of Santa Paula, donated $35,000 toward turning the church kitchen into a legal commercial facility, which was approved by the County of Ventura Environmental Resources.

It is a shame the kitchen isn't getting the use it was, but we are still there for pantry each week and serving more people than ever with more food than imagined.

Staffing the Shelter

Staffing has been our biggest challenge. Because our funding was scarce, we relied on shelter guests for some of the work. Three of them became employees in the early days and due to their own troubled backgrounds, there was always a challenge involving poor judgment, favoritism, food theft and lack of record keeping.

There was a learning curve around when to give people chances and when not to. When you have lived your life creating opportunities for people in your company, it's a major adjustment to figure out new rules for people who have been abused, abandoned, addicted and incarcerated. The potential to become better is in each person, but dealing with the impact and number of adverse childhood experiences is monumental. We will no longer hire a shelter guest. They think they don't have to abide by rules any longer. There is jealousy towards them from other guests, and they stop looking for full-time work so they can move to permanent housing.

Due to a lack of funding, we had not been able to hire a full-time executive director, an additional case manager and a grant writer. I have been working unpaid in the position of director and I am filling in for grant writing, until we can afford to hire someone. However, a new funding agreement with the cities of Santa Paula and Fillmore, matched by the County of Ventura, will keep the shelter in business.

Our neighbors have grown to tolerate us. While our location is away from town, it is on the path of homeless travelers from the river into town. We are next to a very attractive building and there was some discontent about opening without any exterior beautification. Because we are a homeless shelter that opened to fill an emergency need, we promised we would improve our exterior look when we could. We certainly did. The dedication and open house was Aug. 24, 2023—finally.

The opportunity for funding began in September 2022. Our County Supervisor, Kelly Long, and her staff were working closely with us to identify funding to maintain the services. I suggested in one meeting that we contact our state electeds to see what was possible. I took the lead on this effort and sent an email to Assemblymember Steve Bennett. His response was immediate. He asked how much we needed. Early projections were $1.2 million. I asked for $1.5 million. He contacted Sen. Monique Limon and they quickly contacted the budget committee, asking for an 11th hour budget request. It was another miracle. Costs rose dramatically during COVID and the cost was $1.5 million.

Within a few days, the budget was approved and the money was scheduled for transfer to the City of Santa Paula, which would oversee the payments. Finance Director Christy Ramirez and City Manager Dan Singer provided financial oversight. Because we agreed to pay the County's prevailing wage, we have budget overruns and face letting some planned improvements slide to a later date.

On Thursday, April 20, 2023, Southern California Edison arrived as promised at 9 a.m. to turn on the electricity to the new building. We planned to call the addition the *Launch Pad*, because it will house the next initiative to prepare people to live on the outside. We greeted them with balloons and welcome signs. Our dedication and grand opening was August 24, 2023.

I still stand in awe of where and how we started. No one could have planned it the way it all happened. I remember telling then Supervisor Steve Bennett back in 2010 that I had found my life's work.

And I did.

We continue to work hard every day to prevent and end homelessness. There are still many challenges ahead. The greatest are rising rents and the lack of housing for people who are ready to live independently. The other challenges are always reliable funding, shelter safety and sufficient case management to take our guests through the maze of paperwork and the search for permanent housing.

Chapter Three

COVID-19: OUR DAILY COMPANION

Thinking back to March 2020, COVID-19 became the hottest topic. We were early adapters to the warnings, but we were not exempt.

It hit us hard, and it started with the kids around Christmastime of 2019. We just didn't know what it was. The coughing, fever, chills and congestion was worrisome to parents and there were several trips to the emergency room. They always sent them home with Tylenol.

When the official announcement came, we had already experienced a number of cases, and there was soon an outbreak. Our pleas to the public health department were answered, and they became our best partners. Many of our sick ones were put in motels in a nearby community, where they were isolated (alone again) generally for 14 days.

There were rolling infections and outbreaks, so their safe return was uncertain. While some people could test positive for 90 days, symptoms disappeared in others. Everyone was weak and had a hard time completing tasks and chores.

When winter came around in 2021, it was the same experience—and worse in 2022.

Those who heard about our problems were either entirely sympathetic, or not. It's always been odd to realize homeless people are viewed as "less than" and almost untouchable. Any outbreak in any living environment is terribly stressful and worrisome. In 2022, we had 16 kids to care for. Trying to make Christmas a happy event, while risking exposure, was a challenge. That year was worse for adults.

***

In March 2020, we had to close the Drop-In Center. To get an idea of what we were dealing with, check out our Newsletter from that time:

Today, March 23, 2020, we closed the Drop in Center. For nine years, Santa Paula's homeless population has come for coffee, food, restroom breaks, visits with the RISE Team from Behavioral Health and meetings with Case Managers helping with benefits, IDs, health concerns and housing.

We cannot risk exposing our shelter residents to COVID-19. The television was on all day today, grinding home the issues of sheltering in place. We have stopped all visitors and restricted some volunteers from entering the shelter. We have five residents working in essential businesses: agriculture, Spears Mfg and two caregivers. Shelter guests can visit the outdoors and keep doctors' appointments. Fortunately, there are some homeless folks who can literally shelter in place. Thanks to the Presbytery of Santa Barbara, we have installed a portable restroom with handicap access and a handwashing station outside our building for the use of those not allowed inside.

We have a containment pod in the event someone exhibits the signs of the virus. However, we cannot deploy it, because we need an electrical outlet at the exterior of the building and no money to do that.

There is something to be said about learning as you go. It would be impossible to learn everything you need to know about running a shelter before you actually do it. Our great partners in the County CEO's office,

27

the Whole Person Care Division of the Health Care Agency, United Way and Food Share make it all possible.

Safety Protocols in Place

Many Meals will be postponed for a few weeks, but a major food pantry is on as a good substitute. We had many volunteers directing and pacing people. Gloves and masks for everyone in the building.

Food Supply was gone by 5:10 p.m. and we had to restock. We missed week 581—the first time. Social distancing became the byword and the stickers on the concrete every 6 feet are still visible.

We are taking the temperatures of everyone who visits the shelter. Vern Alstot provided us with a Warming Containment Pod onsite. The pod contains two bunk beds and a shower. A portable handicap restroom and handwashing station was donated by the Presbytery of Santa Barbara and set on site to keep them out of the building and let the isolation factor work.

Our food pantry procedures have changed, and it takes many volunteers. All leaders were instructed to space people at 6 feet and pace them entering the building. Volunteers pre-bagged the food to reduce the time facing each other. There was food for 2-3 days. However, without milk, bread and meat, the menus are limited.

We are not allowing visitors in the shelter and everyone washes their hands upon entering the building. So far, no complaints. They know we are protecting them. A Little Laundry has been suspended for a bit.

Shelter guests stay inside to accommodate Governor's orders. "Shelter in Place" has taken on a new meaning in this line of work. We used to have them awaken by 6:30 a.m. each day so they could be out of the building for a while.

We have created space between beds and are alternating head to feet sleeping arrangements so people aren't breathing on each other. We wash sheets and blankets every week. Blanket donations are good!

All New Soap and Sanitizing Systems

This fancy system was installed in our three commercial sinks this week. Two at Harvard and one at the Many Meals church. Soap and rinse water, and sanitizer are all pre-measured to be sure of accuracy.

We have our re-order system in place so we don't run out. We cannot sacrifice any elements of safety at this particular time. Some of the costs to run a shelter are in things you don't know about when planning for funding.

We need an infusion of funding to keep us going on a monthly basis. We have determined we must go year-round, in order to protect both sheltered and non-sheltered populations.

Our Attention on Best Practices to Prevent the Spread of the Current Strain of CoronaVirus

We are taking our cues from the trusted officials at the Ventura County Healthcare Agency and the County CEO's office. We have engaged the services of House Sanitary to assist with the supply and installation of the most effective equipment for food safety and cleanliness. This includes our shelter and the commercial kitchen at the First Presbyterian, where we prepare and serve Many Meals. Robert Ramirez at HD Chem and David Kohlmeier at House Sanitary will be training our service personnel and cooks in best practices.

—Community members can stay informed at Stay Informed by VC Emergency

***

We were an incubator for COVID-19, due to the nature of congregate living.

Harvard Shelter is considered a "low barrier," which means we do not screen as other shelters might. Due to our funding sources with the federal government, we cannot require vaccinations, but we can require masks. Cooperation in this area is minimal at best, because they have to eat and they remove their masks at night.

During 2022 and 2023, we were under construction for the administration wing of Harvard Shelter. COVID slowed down the work. The amazing State Assemblymember, Steve Bennett, in concert with State Senator Monique Limon, petitioned the California State Legislature to provide $1.5 million for building expansion. This request is the result of an email I sent to Assemblymember Bennett, asking if there was funding to expand our building to accommodate more showers and bathrooms, classrooms and office space. It took two weeks for the funding to be approved and two months for funds to arrive in the account of the City of Santa Paula. It took another six months before construction started, and 18 very long months to complete.

As I write this in December of 2023, there is troubling chatter about what is ahead for the coming winter virus games. It's hard to get ready for something not yet named.

Part Two

Realities of Shelter Life

MISSION MATTERS
WE AMPLIFY STORIES

Mr. Century City, LLC

Chapter Four

THINGS TO CONSIDER

Homelessness can be lethal and dangerous, even for those who make it their choice.

Some estimates report that 3,600 homeless people die each year in the United States. The solution seems obvious: Lives would be saved if they slept inside a homeless shelter. But there aren't enough shelter beds to go around, and shelters have rules—often ones they don't like.

1. Many homeless shelters prevent people from spending the day inside.

2. It's difficult working with people to conform to shelter rules. Accommodations must be made.

3. Congregate living brings its own set of problems: Colds and infections are easily spread and irritations can elevate quickly.

4. In today's economy, rising rents have forced people into the streets. Long-term tenants with lower-than-market rents have been forced out to make room for tenants who can pay more. The doors began to close on opportunities.

5. Everyone loves their dog. Homeless people find comfort in their pet and will only go where they can go. Some breeds are more predictable than others, and many owners are not as responsible as the animal deserves. When the animal gets sick, there is pressure on shelter

managers to do something, including managing the flea population and covering vet bills.

6. Substance abuse in any shelter cannot be tolerated for everyone's safety. People with addictions don't do well in the shelter, especially at night.

8. SPIRIT of Santa Paula is the only shelter operator that will take families with kids of all ages. Many limit the ages of boys.

9. Accommodating the new rules for transgender guests is a challenge, but we have managed to do it.

Chapter Five

ROMANCE AT HARVARD SHELTER

There have been numerous romances at Harvard Shelter. It always surprises me how women are content with receiving affection from a man who cannot support them, encourage them or help them be their best selves. They find comfort in sharing a sense of hopelessness and bad habits.

The first time we experienced this was at a winter shelter several years ago in one of our churches. A local mainline church agreed to let us use their storage room for supplies. On two occasions, I was made aware by senior church members that one of my staff members had allowed two different men to stay in the storage room, instead of making them stay at the shelter. I assured them that wasn't possible. I was wrong.

Both men were addicts and both had been in prison, leading the lives homeless men lead. Our female staff member found them more worthy than the others and granted them special privileges, despite all their baggage. She was not long out of that life herself, but had proven to me she was able to handle challenges, based on her own lived experiences. I was wrong about that, too.

That was 12 years ago. Today she is well-employed, a deacon in a local church, married and enjoying life. Both of the men are still homeless.

That act on her part caused a serious breach in my relationship with the church. The members did me a favor by granting use of the room, but they had little use for anyone who was homeless. They had little use for me after that discovery and revoked our right to use the room. This was an early wake-up call to watch for the hazards of dealing with this population.

We've had two pretty serious romantic situations in the shelter. One was Phil, who was released after 17 years in prison. His parents are personal friends of mine. He came out of prison very buff with pythons tattooed on each arm. Jane spotted him the minute he walked through the door.

There is a re-entry program through the County of Ventura, championed by Sandra Lozano. It pays half their salary if they can find a job. Phil was convincing and sincere at the beginning. I hired him as the shelter assistant manager and Jane was also on our payroll, helping us with food rescue. I saw them sneaking kisses on duty and immediately pulled them into my office.

I said, "This has to stop. Staff members cannot do what you're doing." They were good for one day. Then, we caught them in bed together in one of the back rooms on a Tuesday afternoon. I put them on probation saying, "One more violation and you're both going to be fired."

Unfortunately, Phil had a jealous streak and Jane was loving it. She liked to hold her hands up in the air and twirl around in front of him. One night, they were texting each other. He was off duty and she was in bed in the shelter. She was taunting him.

I have copies of their text messages and the language is unbelievable. I cannot use those words in this book. Phil decided he was mad. So, at midnight, he came to Harvard Shelter. He used his key to open the door, walked in, walked over to where Jane was sleeping, and started going through her purse, grabbing things he had given her. They became like two wild people having a confrontation.

My manager called me and said, "You need to get down here." I drove to Harvard at midnight, threw him off the property and fired Jane. I told her, "You're out of here tomorrow."

This is the kind of drama that goes on with people who have not learned how to process their emotions or express their feelings. Instead of saying, "Gee, you really hurt my feelings," Phil grabbed Jane's necklace while rifling through her purse. It wasn't long after that Phil was arrested again for using drugs. Jane went into rehab in Santa Barbara and is doing pretty well. It's unfortunate people have to build up to such a terrible crescendo, in order to realize they are out of control. The worst part is the collateral damage that occurred as people watched Phil, the shelter manager, storm into the building. It was a very upsetting night. As of this writing, Phil is back in prison, due to an incident when he and Jane were together.

Another unlikely romance was between a woman around the age of 50 and a man much younger. She had been cat-fished by an unknown person in an unknown country and was heartbroken. After two years, Diana had been promised a weekend away with him. He sent her pictures from the London airport and as he was landing at LAX, writing that he would see her in two hours. She waited at the curb for six hours, and of course, he never came.

She developed a relationship with at least two of the men at Harvard, citing her desire to have her own sexual needs met. We never knew when these rendezvous would occur, but everyone seemed to know when they did. She would often ask for a weekend pass so she could go to a motel with someone. One day, she asked a shelter manager if a man could die while having sex. We assured her he could.

There were at least two other incidents of relationships that caused Diana to leave Harvard Shelter again. The last go around resulted in us not allowing her to return. She needs drug treatment and will continue to suffer until she completes it.

Then, there's Tanya, who had done everything she needed to do to be granted asylum in the United States. Thanks to great case management, she received her social security card and California ID card, and then found full-time employment.

Also in the building is a very smooth, handsome guy named Anthony, who decided he liked Tanya, even though she does not speak English and he does not speak Spanish. We first noticed something was up when we saw them walking around the property holding hands. I told my staff to keep an eye on them, because she is a staff member and he is not.

One day, Anthony got fired from his job. He's also a meth addict, but Tanya either doesn't believe it or doesn't want to. Meanwhile, she has attached herself to a man who is going nowhere with no obvious future.

People are so hungry for love and affection, they can make poor decisions. One Thursday morning, she was all dolled up after her shift. She looked quite beautiful, like she was going to a fancy party. We saw them walk off the property holding hands.

As I watched this play out in front of me, I realized this girl is headed for disaster. She's going out with an addict who no longer has a job. Fortunately, a church in town has an amazing group of women who are mentors. Two of them adopted her and took her under their wings. They are working to mentor her through this situation, so it doesn't become a disaster.

I really don't want to lose a guest. I have watched her do such good work and it would be awful for her to lose everything over a love affair. But it also reminds me that a shelter is just like every other workplace, where people are looking for love in all the wrong places. These people have all the usual problems and desires, they come with many other complications, too.

When relationships like these develop, there is a tendency for the case manager to face greater challenges. The happier the guest is at Harvard, the less effort they put into securing living accommodations on the outside.

Our case manager has developed a wonderful phrase, encouraging them, "Don't look for love at Harvard; find yourself first."

Challenges That Come with Shelter Romances

Most addicts believe they can stop their substance abuse anytime they want to. If one individual in a relationship is stronger than the other, they will make excuses for why their partner doesn't need treatment. This makes it even more difficult to case manage them. They become codependent and cover each other's tracks so the relationship can continue.

The real challenge is to keep them physically separated in the shelter. Holding hands and kissing leads to gossip and jealousy.

An intriguing part of this is the reminder that we all need some kind of intimate relationship. As of this writing, there isn't a man in Harvard Shelter who can take on the responsibility or the care of another, yet women are still drawn to them.

Many of the women at Harvard have come from abusive relationships. I marvel at their resilience and their willingness to give it another try. Most of the women are mothers and have been responsible for caring for children, even though their own circumstances are challenging. I've often thought they view men as an opportunity to care for someone, which is yet another reason to marvel at human nature.

Parents and Problems with Flirting

Maria called me in September 2022, on a Sunday afternoon. She was sitting in a bus station in Oxnard, which is not our service area. She said, "I got your number from a friend, who said you could help me. I have three daughters with me, and we have nowhere to go." That translates to no one to call and no finances to buy lunch or dinner—homeless. We try to enforce our rules about limiting our services to the Santa Clara Valley, but my mind was focused on a bench in the bus station in Oxnard, with four females with no hope for safety during the night. This is when the "urge to serve" takes over. I said, "Okay, I'll come get you."

Cynthia took the passenger van to get them and found a cute, shapely blonde with blue eyes. Her daughters were 4, 12 and 16. They arrived at Harvard Shelter about 8 p.m. Staff had prepared the containment pod with three bunk beds and everyone was asleep by 9:30 that night.

The four-year-old was a joy. She lit up a room with a sparkle that is hard to describe. She is impish and filled with fun. Mom is very attractive and has been regularly admonished for her provocative clothing and behavior around the men in the room. We came to realize that drug use was a part of her daily life.

The girls were registered for school the next day and settled into a routine. At least one young man in the building took a shine to Maria and found his own self-worth wrapped up in how she treated him. He posted on Facebook a picture of her as his new girlfriend. She was kind to him and he relished it.

Ryan has his own substance abuse problems, and was in no way capable of pursuing a sensible, romantic relationship. His family gave up on him, due to his drug and alcohol use, which created mental incapacity. He's lovable and sweet when he is sober, but there are many reasons why he is at Harvard Shelter.

If Maria talked to another man, he would drink and threaten suicide. If she was not back to the shelter when he thought she should be, it was his excuse to drink. He would be so intoxicated by her return that she pushed him even further away.

As time went by, she became more affectionate toward Ryan and saw him as a sweet brother. He believed they were destined to spend their lives together and they talked about getting an apartment, largely to rescue each other.

Thanks to good case management, Maria was able to gather the paperwork she needed for a successful life outside the shelter. She was hired by a local dentist and the kids were able to go to various childcare opportunities, including the Boys and Girls club after school.

The oldest daughter is very shy and pretty. She took a liking to a young man in the shelter, who was in the same grade at the high school. The mother of the boy was jealous of Maria and refused to allow her son to walk Sophia to school or ride in the same car.

This presented challenges for staff members responsible for getting all the kids to school in the morning. It's terrible to start a day with kids arguing over who has to walk and who gets to ride to school.

It's hard for young girls to learn helpful behaviors when they are watching so many adults exhibit bad ones. We continued to admonish Maria for short skirts and tight pants, but things got better. The men in the building were hoping for some favors. I impress on my staff the importance of using good affirming words, in order to contrast the ever-present language of the street around them.

The food at Harvard is generous and delicious. No one stays at the same weight very long. That solved some of the suggestive clothing problems.

Everything improved when Maria started to work, which proves my continuing reminders to our guests that achieving the life God designed for us includes work!

It's interesting to me that these flirtations take place in a homeless shelter. That's why I say life in a shelter is like almost any neighborhood. This stuff goes on in workplaces and classrooms. Life in the shelter is a microcosm of the world around us.

We've had several women who have come into the shelter thinking it was an open field to find a man. Some will look around a room and think, "I'll take him." There's nothing in it for them. It goes to their world view of surviving day to day. They both want a little love and affection from somebody today that satisfies a need, without worrying about getting saddled with someone who's going to look to them to be the provider. Many are drunk half the time. They've had DUIs. They have no reasonable hope of getting a driver's license or a car.

On another occasion, a cute girl named Lori came into the shelter and started scoping the room for a guy. She picked a couple of them and caused a lot of problems. One of them lost his sobriety over her. He was hurt, cried, started drinking again, and I don't know where he is today. That's a problem in a low-barrier, congregate shelter. We cannot set up hard rules we know would benefit the organization, because Harvard is a low-barrier shelter. We have to take in people who are "homeless." Our only rules for denial are if they are a registered sex offender, have a history of gun violence, have open sores or wounds and cannot care for themselves.

Lori has caused several problems. She has now latched onto a man who is mentally ill. Not dysfunctional, mentally ill. He drinks every day and talks about suicide all the time. He has a picture of himself with Lori on his Facebook page as if she is his girlfriend. When she breaks his heart, I don't know what I'm going to do. And, I can't prevent any of it.

I try to warn the women who come here. I told Lori, "You're cute and there are people here who will find you attractive. There are young women in the building watching you and your behavior. It's up to you to set a good example for them and not break somebody's heart." Of course, their big problem on the outside is also often the affairs and love triangles they create.

But alas! We now have a married couple Cheryl and Darryl, experiencing homelessness due to job loss, high rents and a lot of bad luck. He is working at Spears Manufacturing. Dr. and Mrs. Cooper are donating their used car to them to make it easier to get around. They attend the Presbyterian Church and prove if there is a will, there is a way. Absent substance abuse, they are able to handle their homelessness strategically and successfully.

These stories support my observation that everyone needs somebody to love and to love them. A shelter environment is not a place where success is rampant, so bits and pieces of affection will do. And, of course, the human condition is such that people are attracted to other people for a variety of reasons. Because they live in close proximity to each other, there is a camaraderie that is hard to explain. Almost every known emotion floats through the room on a daily basis.

If love is in the air, that is the good news—and the bad.

Chapter Six

BOYS WILL BE BOYS

Jay and John embody a study on how much trouble two teens can get into and how likable they can be at the same time.

Somewhere in history, someone thought the phrase "boys will be boys" would be the ultimate excuse for the childish behavior of men at any age. In a homeless shelter, that phrase is almost a death sentence for young men who have experienced every adverse childhood experience possible. The expectation for them to "get it" and become responsible adult men is unrealistic.

Several years ago, a deputy with the Public Defender's Office asked me if I would shepherd a young woman with six children. I agreed to help. There were five girls and one boy. The mom accused the son of molesting his sisters and claimed the father raped her in front of the children. I bought her a car, a bed, groceries and helped out with rent. It turned out she was lying to me the entire time. She had a boyfriend. And the father of her children was the brother of a close friend, who assured me none of it ever happened.

I was able to help this woman get a car so she could go back-and-forth to work. She had an accident on the freeway and it was a total loss. I learned recently a client of mine knew her in a different setting and she also provided her with a car.

This mother sent her then 10-year-old son to live with a relative in Las Vegas. Several days went by without her hearing from him. She told me he had been kidnapped and insisted she must drive to Vegas to find out for herself what had happened to him.

I rented a car for her to get John. The kidnapping was also not true. She went there to have a weekend with her boyfriend. Then, she brought her son back to Santa Paula, where he went to live with a relative.

At the age of 19, John was homeless and arrived back at Harvard Shelter. I thought he looked familiar, but I did not mention it. That too can be an adverse experience if it's tied to some other event. He did not graduate from high school and instead of enrolling in continuation school, he spends his days at the local gym. That's John.

Now for Jay.

Back when Harvard Shelter first opened, a social worker colleague in Fillmore asked if I would take in a "nice young kid." His name was Jay and he was 18 at the time. He came in withdrawn, sullen, a face full of acne and did not communicate with anyone. He just sat on his bed with his phone and was kind of mysterious. Looking in the face of today's mass shootings by angry young men, this kid fit the profile perfectly.

One day, we learned he had a gun in his possession in the shelter and, at the same time, we got an alert about a shooting threat at both Santa Paula and Fillmore high schools.

The threats were traced to Jay. A swarm of officers descended on our shelter and took him to jail. He eventually got out, but had nowhere to go. His mother was an addict living in her car, so there was no help or accountability there.

Three years later, Jay called and asked if he could return to Harvard. He had not been in any trouble since then, so I agreed to meet up and talk.

He had definitely matured, and it became apparent his old behavior was a part of his history. He came in and shortly afterward, John came in. They quickly became buddies and we learned they are actually cousins.

Adverse experiences continued to follow Jay. While he was not especially uncooperative, he did not communicate well with staff and avoided completing assignments. Somehow, he managed to finish his GED, but he has no desire to work.

We gave him a chance as a SPIRIT employee, helping load and unload food from the grocery stores back to Harvard. We also hired John to help with those tasks. When Jay and John were together, they were worthless as employees, and the F-word was their byword. Both were disrespectful to staff and argumentative.

Soon, a 15-year-old girl named Julie appeared at Harvard Shelter. She gave every impression of being at least 25 years of age. We did not know she was Jay's girlfriend out on the streets. When she heard Jay was back at Harvard Shelter, she pretended to be homeless and came in. We later learned that she filed charges against him for rape, which is an even more serious crime, because she is under 18 years of age. He denied all the allegations, although many subsequent text messages revealed a different story. Her story appears later in this book, under "Dangerous Friends."

It wasn't long before the work product of both young men became so intolerable, I could not justify keeping them on the payroll. They received two violations for being sassy with the supervisors, so they knew they were on thin ice with me. They were disrespectful to staff and the F-word continued to be their first choice for expletives. During a drug sweep with the police canine, we found bags of weed in their possession. That was the last straw. While it's legal in California, it is considered contraband inside the shelter and against the rules.

I went to Harvard the next morning, and in my calmest voice, told them how disappointed I was in their deception, however, I wanted nothing but the best and success for them. I calmly terminated them both and asked them to turn in their SPIRIT shirts and their timesheets. I told them I'd have a check for them by 3 p.m., and asked if they had any questions for me.

"Nope." I handed them their paychecks without a word. They hung their heads and left the room.

One weekend, Jay asked if he could have an overnight so he could babysit a friend's dog while they were out of town. Normally, we require a 48-hour notice, but I chose to believe him and granted the overnight.

The next morning, two officers came to Harvard looking for Jay, who happened to be in the building. They examined the sign-in sheets to determine if he was in the building when a robbery occurred in Fillmore, known as a beer run.

Because he had properly signed in and out, we could demonstrate where he was. However, the next day, the deputies returned with Jay's picture on camera at the scene of the crime. The deputies left, but later obtained a warrant for his arrest. When the officers arrived, he jumped the fence and ran away. He called me later that evening and asked if he could come back to Harvard when he was released from jail. I assured him he could. His court date for the rape charge was on the 17th and he wanted to evade police until then. At the age of 20, he is now charged with both rape and robbery. He will do time for one or the other, or both.

I attended his court appearances and both were continued to a later time. His mother finally bailed him out of jail. I would not.

His absence from Harvard Shelter created a bed for someone else, but he would take a different bed in the system. The funny street line is that "three hots and a cot" is all they care about.

There is sorrow in realizing how the generational impact of adverse childhood experiences cripples young men and women. What kind of parents will they be? What is the future for their children? Soon, we will be looking at three generations of poverty, limited education and meager earning potential. There will be limited contributions into the social security system from these very lost people, and those of us who plan on retiring may have to work longer to pay for their care.

Providing food and shelter is not enough. Being kind and loving is not enough. At least it doesn't appear that way today. Case management is essential and includes many of the elements of parenting.

Maybe they will remember the good part of our care and we will have given them enough strength to leave the little boy behind and eventually grow up. Boys need to learn to be men before they can grow into one. Who will show them?

As of Sept. 5, 2023, both John and Jay are in jail for firing a firearm and contributing to the delinquency of a minor.

Chapter Seven

THE IMPORTANCE OF CASE MANAGEMENT

At 8 a.m. on a Sunday morning, a woman called, stating she was homeless and had no more money for a motel. She had six children and the youngest two were autistic, needing special schools. She was out of money for food, and she was crying, desperate, feeling depressed and lost. She found me on the internet. She was also fleeing a domestic violence matter in another state.

I drove to Simi Valley that morning and met her and all six, sweet kids at the motel and paid for a few more nights of lodging. It was my day to do the food rescue run to Albertsons in Newbury Park, so the timing was perfect.

We started with case management. Vern Alstot made a referral to the One Stop meeting in Ventura on that Tuesday. I met her and her 20-year-old daughter at 8:30 a.m., and returned them to the motel at 2:30 that afternoon. They registered for Medi-Cal, Cal Fresh, entered into HMIS and met with the case managers from Whole Person Care and Human Services. The next day, the case manager met with her at the motel, paid for a few more nights and arranged for a different motel room with a kitchen in a nearby town, near a school that welcomes kids with autism.

It took a team of 20 people to make this happen. Case management is essential and the odds of getting this type of work done without it are staggeringly low. Kids need stability and their parents need to be settled. The next step is employment, securing day care, ensuring reliable transportation and having permanent supportive housing. That is the biggest challenge of all. All this happened, thanks to Jennifer Harkey and James Boyd at Whole Person Care. One down, thousands to go.

This is when you calculate the human rate of return on an investment of a few nights in a motel. It secured them, brought peace to the family and bought us the time we needed to mobilize services. That rate of return is priceless.

In 2023, the Gene Haas Foundation blessed us with a generous donation of $35,000 for the work of SPIRIT of Santa Paula. This money helped us to stabilize our case management program designed to take our guests through the process of getting ready to leave Harvard. Our biggest challenge continues to be finding suitable housing that takes people from the streets and our shelter to their permanent home. Our friends at the Gene Haas Foundation encouraged us to stay the course and look everywhere for a "win."

Bank of the Sierra also stepped in with a check for $40,000 to keep our doors open. Their banking motto is to make the community better wherever they do business. They certainly did that for us.

Career Crashes

Charlotte was credentialed to teach in five subjects and taught in a famous Catholic school in the east. She had wealthy parents, never married and her siblings rejected her through the process of her unraveling, during significant health challenges. At the age of 60, she had a pretty good retirement income, but was unmanageable and angry most of the time. She lashed out at people, and conversations quickly turned to sarcasm and putdowns. She was smart and argued better than anyone.

Charlotte encountered us several times before coming to Harvard. The first time was when she was ready to move out of Fillmore, where she was renting a room. Someone told her to call me to help her move. It turned out to be more than just a bed—it was enough furniture for a small house. Some of her furniture had to be left at the curb. We helped her move into an apartment where she was forced to stay outside the house all day. The primary tenant moved a family member into her room. It was a nightmare for her.

Her career had been fabulous during her life, and she complained when I referred to her as retired. She said, "I'm not retired. I'm going back to work." But due to physical and mental challenges, probably caused by some adverse childhood experience that manifested itself as an adult, her life unraveled. Everything kept getting worse and she continued to insist she was going back to work. However, there was no way. Her health was not good, nor was her emotional state.

Fortunately, Jessica Lucas was her case manager, who took her by the hand and got her the doctors she needed. Jessical was relentless. Peter Lemmon is a local lawyer, who contacted her family when her mother died and secured her inheritance. The case manager eventually got her into a retirement facility in Pasadena, which is where she will spend the rest of her life—safe and secure. We hear she is happy.

This is an all-too-common story about how a person collapses, because they don't have stabilizing pillars to prop them up when things don't go right. When you don't have a family member or close friend to rely on, you can fall apart. At 65, you're supposed to have it together, so your retirement years are not spent in a homeless shelter.

We have had others who had great jobs, but crashed their careers, due to substance abuse, significant health challenges or emotional instability.

Refusing Help

A young mom called me at 10 p.m. on a Wednesday night, saying she just got kicked out of her house. She said, "My baby's dad doesn't want us to live at the house anymore. He wants us to leave and I have nowhere to go." She was sobbing. I asked where she was. She stated she was in the house. He wanted her to leave. I said, "Here's what you do. Go to him and say you found someone who's going to help, but she can't do it until tomorrow morning, and you need to stay here tonight. Tell him, "Tomorrow morning, I'll be gone.""

She said, "But what if he won't let me?" I urged her to try. She took a deep breath and asked him to allow them to stay. There was nothing I could do at 10 p.m., short of a call to police for a welfare check. She didn't want that. If I went to get them and put them in a motel, then I would be troubled when I got home, wouldn't be able to sleep and I'd be exhausted the next day.

I met with her the next morning at my office. She said, "He's calling and he wants me to go back with him." I warned her that returning would be asking for more of the same kind of medicine she got the night before. "He doesn't love you. He doesn't care about the baby. Take this as an opportunity to go start your life over," I said. She left.

I heard from her two days later. She went back to him as she had many times before. She also had a family who begged her not to go back to him. What a pattern. She is a pretty woman of about 25 years old with a baby.

51

I called the county and asked what happens to people like this. They said, "They call people like you." I asked, "So what do you do for them?" They said, "We refer them to people like you."

People in these situations can call Homeless Services and leave a message. They will be called back the next day. There is no urgent response unless it is to 911. It can take days to get any help. I get so tired of hearing this.

To get permanent housing, the person has to find a rental, which means she has to have a job, an income, a decent credit score and good rental history before a landlord will rent to anyone. Then, there's Rapid Rehousing. That's a complete misnomer. There's no such thing as Rapid Rehousing.

Indispensable Guidance

In 2016, the Harbor Church in Ventura was located close to a school and they decided to start serving the homeless people. They went through terrible wars with their neighbors. I remember the dedicated and passionate pastor, Sam Gallucci. He was quoted in the newspaper saying, "We will not do case management, because that's not the role of the church." However, in reality, it is. We are to guide. We are to lead. We are to teach and encourage. That's what case management is. If he had instead said, "We are going to get two case managers right now," he would probably still be there. Sam was an early adapter to serving people experiencing homelessness. He was brave and passionate. He encouraged me to stay the course.

Case management is essential to this work. If we don't do case management, our guests will still be lying in bed 10 years from now. It's not only about giving them food and a place to sleep. We are obligated to help them get on with their lives. Unfortunately, some of them really don't want to.

Case Management Increases Success

We have experienced many success stories as a result of
case management. Some people need more than others. Some
automatically disqualify themselves if they choose to remain in their
addiction. Is sobriety hard? Absolutely. Is sobriety worth it? No
question.

Assuming someone is ready for a life change, there are many steps to
launching out of Harvard. What is simple and second-nature for most
of us is complicated and confusing to others. Life on the street warps
reality and many become satisfied with very little.

Homelessness also results in losses. No documents, no phone, no
contact numbers, confusion and irritation. Case management begins
with baby steps and Plan A, which lays out tasks and expectations
for six months. Once they experience even a small success, such as
getting their photo ID, they are motivated to go for the next document.
The goal is to get everyone ready to move out of Harvard Shelter.
That requires a job, a savings account and lots of documentation.

Case Manager Losses

Our successes typically coexist with their opposites. To that end,
there is a danger lurking in the life of every case manager and that
danger is wanting more for their clients than their clients want for
themselves. Jessica Lucas was our first case manager who came to us
from Mercy House with experience both in the workplace and in her
personal life, with a brother who was homeless.

She was driven to make magic happen for those who would
cooperate. When there was a failure, she took it as her own. She could
not let any success substitute for lack of one.

Because she knew she had to take care of herself, she left us after only a year. Jessica changed the outcome of life for many who are now permanently and safely housed. Joy and sorrow should not be comrades, but they seem to be in the world of case management. However, she has returned to us part-time with renewed enthusiasm and knowing better how to take care of herself. She is immersed in her master's degree work and this creates the opportunity for work in her required internship.

Getting Your Face Right

At staff meetings, we talk about how to do better, how to be better, be kinder, love more and keep ourselves from becoming cynical.

The behavior inside Harvard affects all of us—more often in negative ways than in positive ones.

For example, an adult child who was almost 50 years old told his mother he could not get out of bed until he had a piece of cake. What to do? It was 9 a.m. on a Sunday morning. And then it was noon.

Mom pleaded with staff to provide cake for her son. Viewing ice cream as a greater food value, we offered a pint of rich strawberry. He declined and said it had to be cake.

At 5:30 p.m., he insisted he still couldn't get out of bed until he had cake. This mother's enabling didn't start when they arrived at Harvard Shelter. Meanwhile, an argument started between the guests and a staff member who was accused of causing stress in their lives and not caring about their well-being. Leanna was accused of depriving them of simple pleasures and being selfish. She was told she was a loser and needed to get a job somewhere else. Actually, she has another job. She is a case manager for Child Protective Services for the County of Ventura.

When I arrived that night for the mandatory Sunday House Meeting, Leanna asked to speak to me privately. She began to cry, feeling overwhelmed by the insanity of demanding cake, the hurtful accusations and the refusal to cooperate.

She wondered how she could continue doing the work and what others would think of her if she gave in—or didn't.

Leanna has her own world of lived-experiences that can easily bubble up in moments of pressure and stress. Old behaviors come to mind, which can influence good judgment and responses, when trauma-informed care is needed the most.

It takes a strong, sweet person to breathe deeply and step back, not letting others' emotions control hers so she can maintain her position as manager, yet respond in the manner we expect of our guests.

It sounds simple, doesn't it?

It isn't simple. By its very nature, it's very hard. This type of work brings out the best and the worst of both staff and guests. Even on everyone's days of best behavior, every emotion is close to the surface. The topics of fairness are regularly thrown about the room, even their perceived entitlements, despite their personal circumstances.

We find most people want to make sense of their day, and most really want the day to count for something. I've read where people make 35,000 decisions a day. Imagine that! I wonder if many of our guests make even a dozen decisions a day—good or bad.

Leanna stopped to think about her role as manager of the fragile and needy, and how she could regain solid footing. She questioned her ability to do the job. When I convinced her of her skills, value and merits, she took a few moments to gather her thoughts, but she was afraid to face the room again, until she could "get her face right." She knew she would reflect her own emotions, even though she didn't want to.

"Getting our face right" can be accomplished when our heart is right with the world. Knowing what we do matters for today and for eternity. It helps us do what we need to do and reach a little higher to do even more.

Trauma-informed care is a wonderful way to live your life. If you are unfamiliar with that term, it refers to a way to approach people with a history of trauma, such as abuse or violence, with sensitivity and compassion. It involves asking permission, offering empathy and finding support. It works in marriages, families and workplaces. We assume everyone we meet has been traumatized in some way. We practice using words that do not re-traumatize. We ask questions instead of making demands. We do better on some days than we do on others.

Practice helps us keep our faces right.

The House Meeting started promptly at 7 p.m. As far as I could tell, both Leanna and I were wearing our "right" faces.

Essential and Indispensable

Case management provides such a crucial role in addressing the complex needs and challenges faced by individuals experiencing homelessness. Each individual requires a personalized assessment to identify the root causes of their situation, and identify their unique needs and goals which may include housing assistance, mental health services, addiction treatment, job training, medical care and/or other support services.

Case managers act as coordinators, connecting people with service providers, agencies and community resources. They ensure individuals receive services that are tailored to their needs, reducing duplication and ensuring efficient resource utilization. They make and track many appointments for their clients. Some are video conferences, some are in person or three-way calls. It's a lot.

Case managers also serve as advocates, helping the homeless people navigate complex systems, access benefits and secure essential resources. They also provide emotional support, guidance and encouragement, which helps people build self-confidence and resilience. They are an essential component of increasing successful outcomes for the homeless population.

The hidden, but crucial challenge comes when assigned tasks are not completed. It's hard to hear someone say, "That's your job, not mine." Sigh.

Chapter Eight

GENERATIONAL KNUCKLEHEADS

Our two young friends at the shelter, Jay, 19, and John, 22, have equal ability to avoid telling the truth. They learned the skill from their parents. We also have a 14-year-old girl at the shelter, named Lisa, who stayed home from school again today, because ... it's raining.

She is insolent, lazy, hateful, mean and rude. Her mother rolls her eyes, and asks, "What can I do?" Her mother lives at Harvard and all she wants is a man. She is constantly looking around the room to see who is new and might be just right for her.

It's disconcerting to watch the patterns that evolve in kids who are lazy. They lie easily and they believe their own lies. John recently got COVID-19 and was placed into a hotel room by the county. His buddy, Jay, told the staff, "I want to spend the night with my mom." Even though they are supposed to give a 48-hour notice to go stay with a parent, we always say yes to that request. We found out later, Jay went to the hotel room where John was staying and spent the night.

I knew they were together, so I called the hotel room and asked John if Jay was there. He said, "No." I asked if Jay spent the night in his hotel room and they both were quiet. They were trying to figure out what to say. Jay chimed in, "No." I told them I knew they were lying to me, because the hotel manager said they were there. It got very quiet again. So, I repeated, "Did you spend the night?" He said, "Yeah, I guess so."

This type of behavior is generational. I watch kids who come in with their parents and mimic their bad behavior. These kids know it's bad. How will we ever correct that? We've had many families where the behavior of the kids is just like that of their parents. I don't know how to reprogram the pattern of laziness. As long as they stay sheltered and have a warm bed, blankets, clothes and some food, there's no incentive to do anything with their lives.

Lisa stayed home from school for the second day in a row. I talked to her mom. I'm learning to tone it down and be sympathetic, instead of being authoritarian by saying, "Marissa, I'm really concerned about Lisa." She replied, "Yeah, why?" I responded, "She's been home for two days sick." She said, "Oh yeah, she doesn't want to go to that school anymore. We're gonna put her in Vista Real," which is an independent school for kids who can't conform to a classroom.

I didn't believe her. So, I called the school. They couldn't tell me much, but we've worked together before. I asked, "Can you tell me if Lisa is starting school with you on Monday?" They said, "Well, she has an interview with us on Thursday." That means, she's not planning on going to school on Monday, Tuesday and Wednesday.

When Lisa came to us last year, she was 14 going on 15, and struggling in school. We planned to give her a Quinceanera, a Mexican-American tradition of celebrating a girl's 15th birthday, marking the transition from childhood to young womanhood. But I told her we needed a contract if we were going to do this. In exchange for the party, she was to go to a weekly *Ignite* meeting at a local church, read a book a week and a few other things. She gladly signed it. The first week, I asked her how she liked *Ignite*. She said, "Oh I didn't go." What happened? "I didn't want to go." I asked, "What about our contract?" She replied, "I don't care. Do what you want."

When she knew I was serious, we re-started the contract and she began asking about when we were going to order her dress. I explained it was too early. Next year, she might be a different size. The agreement started to break down again and she refused to do any of her chores. She wouldn't even take a shower. One day, she came home with very long fake eyelashes and artificial nails. Parents often reward their kids with these things so they don't feel different from other kids, thinking they will behave better and be happier. It's not working.

I called this section Generational Knuckleheads, but it's also about laziness and complacency. And, perhaps, it's about loss of hope. They believe they have no future and it's too hard to get one. They have not learned that working is how we all get through life.

Jay and John love having paychecks. The case manager has developed a system to help them save money and acknowledge the good reasons for doing so. They would not have initiated that on their own.

We have a whole generation of kids like these three. They're on their cellphones and TikTok much of the day and night, while living in a shelter and modeling their parents' bad behavior.

I don't know what the future holds for them, and for those of us who are productive adults. What's going to happen to the gross national product? Clearly, there are Gen Xers who are working hard. But many of the Millennials and Gen Zs are falling apart at the seams. Many productive adults will have to work longer and retire later to provide for the generation following us. I hope there's a balance in this generation.

We're not the only homeless shelter in the United States facing these issues. Kids in foster care can fall into this pattern as well. Some do well, but they're the lucky few. It takes extreme motivation and work to recover from patterns of laziness.

Chapter Nine

THE TERRORIST IN THE ROOM

This is a regular phenomenon at shelters and in jails and, to a certain extent, in many organizations. When someone enters with a bold personality, it doesn't take long before they start to intimidate others and control the space.

One such guest at Harvard was a man named Adrian, who came to live in our shelter. He started dogging me on Facebook and threatening me. We had to dismiss him not long after his arrival. One night, a mother accused a guest of "touching" her young son. Adrian decided to take on the accusation, and he and another assaulted the guest. Police were called and the cameras examined. There was no touching and no charges. The mother apologized. Adrian never believed it and never stopped talking about it on social media.

Adrian was threatening, argumentative and scary. He had a prison background and restraining orders from his own family. His siblings acted similarly.

It's interesting how these behaviors evolve. They come in very sweet, nice, asking how they can help. They're so grateful. But when they get comfortable and feel like they have us swooning, they start to take over. They want to change the dinner hour, control the TV remote, change the shower schedule, re-write chores and refuse to follow rules they deem foolish—like signing out and signing in. Then, they begin the authority challenge, often first thing in the morning, last thing at night or at the dinner hour. This behavior disrupts the house. It's hard for staff to maintain calm within themselves and those around them.

You know what they say about one bad apple. In prisons, they call them "shot-callers," where a tough guy elevates himself to own the jail. He calls the shots. He decides who lives, who suffers and even who dies.

We have them at Harvard Shelter, and they are all ages and genders. It's clear why many of them are homeless, and they are on the spectrum of dangerous and hopeless.

There's the mom living in her car with three kids, because dad got a girlfriend and kicked them out. There are ones who just got out of prison. They know what kind of story to tell so they can ingratiate themselves and get comfortable. Then, they can start operating their business again. Their business is terrorizing people, selling drugs and manipulating the environment so even someone like me can sense danger and fear.

We give so many chances to people so they can get it right. They trick us, by pretending to be kind and helpful. However, as soon as they get comfortable and a foothold, they start taking over the environment. They manipulate and scare people into silence and submission, so they can run the room. What they don't realize is there's nothing to run. It's a homeless shelter. But for them, if they're the boss of the room, they have achieved success, acceptance and privilege. They soon learn I am the boss without fear, and am relentless and committed to peace and safety.

A shelter is like any neighborhood in any city. There are people who spoil the environment, are troublemakers, manipulators, givers and takers. There are also some happy people who look forward to each day. There are participants with hope. People with all types of personalities can, and do, end up in shelters. They have to be managed so they don't take over and everyone feels safe. The challenge for staff is to manage the extremes and not neglect those in the middle.

Volunteers and Mentors

Sometimes we host well-meaning members of the community who volunteer at the shelter. I ask about their lived experience, if any. If they don't know what I mean by that, we need advance preparation for their visit.

Volunteers can be easily manipulated by house guests. We tried a mentoring program with a local organization, and the result of most efforts was guests asking for gifts, money and favors. It's a talent to say "no" and smile at the same time. The greater talent is to stick to it.

One of the more disappointing elements of mentoring is the slide of guests from initial enthusiasm to disinterest, when they learn the benefits of the relationship are limited to thoughtful and careful conversations.

Many of our guests come to an understanding of our good intentions and deep relationships. Like any neighborhood, some guests stay silent, some work at getting what they can with as little effort as possible. Some will let everyone else do their work, and some will do the minimum to get by. You know, like any neighborhood.

That's why all our managers and supervisors have lived experience. They cannot be manipulated. They know the drill and can spot this behavior developing across the room.

The opposite of the terrorists in the room are the fragile, shy and vulnerable. But even they have their moments.

Chapter Ten

FRAGILE AND VULNERABLE

It was a cool and cloudy Saturday morning at Harvard Shelter, when Leanna, one of our staff members, took Clara to Camarillo to retrieve the last of her personal belongings. She and her 42-year-old son, Ralph, were evicted from a home, where she said they lived with her fiancé.

Clara is 72 years old and Ralph is a priest in an orthodox church with attachments to the Gideons and other religious organizations. They are used to sitting at the head of the table. When they learned I was the Executive Director, they huddled around me to begin an exchange about important ideas and world events.

Both are gentle, kind and vulnerable to all negative elements of the world. They are highly educated and it seems like they don't belong at Harvard.

They have no resources, support or family, but they toss around the names of well-known locals as though they have been best friends. They claim a local farming family put a $50,000 check in their mailbox, but someone intercepted it and cashed it.

Ralph suffers from a genetic disorder, which affects the connective tissue that supports and anchors your organs and other structures in the body. This makes him very weak with low energy. They came to us while they were living in their car in Fillmore. It was filled with important and historic documents. They are timid and Clara claimed they were entitled to an $85,000 inheritance from her husband's insurance policy, which was due any day.

A trip to the investment company revealed that to be true, but the account manager at Fidelity Investments in Thousand Oaks was not impressed by them, nor was he anxious to be of service. It took three trips with me to straighten out the account with the help of a supervisor. It was frustrating to watch the sloppy manner of a disinterested young account manager work through the complexities of getting the policy redeemed and into a bank account.

The eviction attorney only gave Clara a 24-hour notice to retrieve everything from the house they were renting. We are short staffed on Saturdays, but Leanna agreed to take Clara in the passenger van while Maria filled in as supervisor. I took the food rescue run to free up personnel.

Their story goes to the heart of tragedy that occurs when people have no resources. When there is no one to call and no back up, they go to the streets.

We also learned, it would cost almost $1,000 to get their car registered. It has not been registered since 2019. This meant the car was subject to being towed if it sat on a city street. Due to our construction, there was no room to park on site. They were featured in one of our newsletters, and several people provided financing to solve their immediate problems.

Efforts at getting their car registered were stalled, because the car needed to have a favorable smog test and it failed. Ralph insisted they take the car to a Dodge dealer 40 miles away, because the diagnostic test would be more reliable, and repairs done by the dealership would be under warranty.

A reliable company here in Santa Paula was capable of the same thing, but they felt they needed to go to the Dodge dealership. There was no appointment for days, meanwhile they would run the risk every day of the car being towed. I was prepared to take this decision out of their hands, because time was of the essence.

People who have been used to taking care of business, but have lost control of their lives, can become combative when we try to solve their problems the easy way and the decision is no longer theirs to make. I had to exert my authority, because others were paying for this remedy. The work could be done locally, but the car is still not registered, because Ralph's license expired.

In many ways, they are a pitiful partnership because, while they rely on each other, each is of little help. His illness requires sleep and rest and he stays medicated. She is the hovering mother and protects him in every way possible. While we typically separate men and women, we allow these two to sleep side-by-side. She is the ever-protective mother looking after her fragile chick.

Fortunately, there was no rain on the day they went to pick up their belongings. When Clara and Leanna arrived at the house, their property sat in the driveway, including a new mattress. Most of it was trash and unknown items in boxes. All items, useful or not, were moved into the van and they traveled back to Santa Paula. I met them when they arrived. Ralph was still in bed and had difficulty waking. I looked at this 40-year-old, fragile son and felt such a wave of pity.

We parked their vehicle and the passenger van in the parking lot, and let them spend the afternoon going through the boxes. Some of it ended up in the trunk of their car and the rest went into the trash.

This is a sad commentary for a once-productive family to end their lives, sheltering with 47 other people, wondering how they will fare in the end. In reality, each day becomes part of the end of their story.

We are here to help write their story in the most compassionate way possible. I dread the day they become separated, for the other will be truly left behind in a very fragile state.

Thanks to intensive case management from Sabriana and my oversight, we were able to secure permanent housing for them in Ventura, thanks to Project RoomKey, a project of the County of Ventura Continuum of Care, managed by Jennifer Harkey. They are near services and even though they share a room and bathroom, they enjoy the fresh air from the beach and the sound of the train that runs within yards of their windows.

While most of us would not want to live out our lives in a motel room, the needs and the expectations of homeless people become simple, as do the things that become precious.

We are still their case managers and provide the services they need. They have become experts at Uber, DoorDash, online banking and internet capabilities. His dreams include returning to his studies and ministry. Clara just wants to be his mom and keep him safe. As of September 2023, the car is still not registered, and Ralph does not have his driver's license. However, all of his fancy and scholarly books are neatly lined on the shelf in their closet. They are comforted just by looking at them.

Their story reveals why it is important to note the many reasons for homelessness.

Chapter Eleven

THE MASTER MANIPULATOR

Marco arrived in Santa Paula in about 2016. He is the cousin of a very well-known family in Santa Paula. He grew up here, then moved to Oregon. When he came back, no one would let him in their house, but they all told him to "Go see Kay." Marco was smart, very capable and a smooth talker. He was also a meth addict. I didn't see that at first, so I let him live at my office until I started seeing the signs of late night activities, as well as disassembled appliances and equipment.

One night around midnight, he wanted to clean out the garage. My office was downtown, so the police were watching. He had a cute little dog who had puppies at our winter shelter. His girlfriend was in another state. He stole her car, but he kept telling me she promised to get the car registered in his name, so he could drive it without a problem. He stayed at the shelter, where he suffered from terrible tooth pain. I used to pick him up and take him to the hospital, but the only thing they would do is give him meds for the infection.

He went through a lot of money. I used to take him to work in Ventura, because his car was impounded. He eventually got it back, but he never did have a California license or register the car. He had all the complications of a person living a screwed-up life. He called one day to ask if I would help him with rent. He found a room to rent in Ojai and needed $180. I told him I could only give the money to the landlord. He said, "I don't want the landlord to know I can't make the rent." I told him I was not going to give him cash, and if he wanted me to pay his rent, it would go to the landlord. What's her name, I asked? He gave me a name, but he never picked up the check.

Back in 2018, he arrived at the shelter with an adorable little dog named Sparkle. She was a homely little thing, but attractive to a handsome little Pomeranian and became pregnant. Sparkle eventually had three beautiful puppies. They were a major attraction at the winter shelter. Relatives allowed Marco to stay with them (and the Pomeranian) for a couple of weeks when he first arrived in Santa Paula. However, he was apparently stealing money, which is why he was asked to leave.

Marco was good at getting jobs. He worked for roofing companies that transported him to various job sites. He needed someone to watch the puppies during the day. I finally insisted the puppies had to be adopted out, as we were closing the winter shelter soon. Marco cried. We got them adopted through a local pet rescue foundation and Marco suffered from the loss.

Fast forward three years, he was back asking for help. He called and asked if he could meet with me. He came to my office with a girl he introduced as Charlotte, from Oregon. This was the girl from whom he stole the car. They decided to reconcile, because she was now here. I asked what he wanted. He said, "Can we borrow $500 so we can rent a room?" I said, "No. I'm not helping you." It's hard for me to say no, but Marco had received more than his share of help and support. It's one of those "enough already" moments.

One day, Marco hit another car at the shopping center. With no tags on the car and no driver's license, he found himself in trouble. When I showed up, Marco said, "Thank you, Kay, for coming." The officer asked, "Is Kay helping you?" He said, "Yes." Then, the officer turned to me and said, "Are you really helping him?" I responded that I was trying to. So, they let him go and let him keep the car.

Another night, Marco got arrested and the arresting officer called me from the station. He said, "Do you know a guy named Marco (with his last name)?" I said, yes. He said, "He has a little dog." I said, "Yes, that's Sparkle."

The officer asked if I would get the dog. When I walked into the booking station, I saw Marco holding Sparkle and he was sitting on the floor with her. I called her name and she ran right to me. She knew there was trouble. When she jumped up into my arms, the officer said, "Take her." So, I kept Sparkle for two weeks until Marco got out of jail. It was hard to return the dog to him.

This is a model of the collapsing economy people live in. It's one step forward and two steps back. When I told him I wouldn't give him the $500 for the room rental, he left mad. The girlfriend was really mad, because I think I embarrassed her by calling her out about the car. They ended up living in that same car outside Harvard Shelter, coming in for food every day. I think she left him, and he disappeared for a while.

That's the tragedy of people who have no focus, no purpose and are addicts. They can't think clearly. They can't plan, and their lives fall apart.

These events are woven into all of the stories of addicts. It gets old and exhausting, even talking about it, because it feels so hopeless. However, I recently saw Marco at Catalyst Church two weeks in a row. There is hope. I have to remember that myself.

I intentionally spoke to him and asked after him and Sparkle. Marco saw this gesture as a rekindling of an opportunity. He called a few days later, asking for a meeting, because he had a need and an idea. I did not call him back.

I worry more about them than they do. When I don't see someone for a period of time, they pop up here or there. I assume they made it somehow, somewhere. They do, sometimes, and more often than not.

Chapter Twelve

THE FOOD RESCUE OP

One great day in September 2017, I received a call from Silvia Lopez-Navarro, at Ventura County Public Health, asking if SPIRIT would be interested in participating in a food rescue program designed to keep food from the landfills. We were all in for that opportunity. Community Action of Oxnard was also included in the invitation.

It began in earnest when Dr. Robert Levin, Director of Public Health, called a meeting of interested parties. Included in the meeting were various agencies, including food rescue expert Mike Learakos of Waste Not, Orange County. He was the owner of Katella Grill in Anaheim. He closed the restaurant right after the pandemic ended, and has become an authoritative expert and consultant on food rescue. His food rescue sources were Disneyland and Angel Stadium. Imagine that.

***

Here is the email invitation of Friday, September 8, 2017:

Dear Ventura County colleague,

I think we can all agree that it is a worthy goal to feed the hungry in our county and to decrease food waste. Public Health has initiated an exploratory effort to create an initiative in Ventura County, which aims to achieve these two ends. Successful programs such as this already exist. One such innovative program is Waste Not, Orange County. In the next couple of weeks, Public Health will host an informational meeting for those who are involved with food production or provision, and numerous other entities, which deal with food waste. You and your organization have been identified as a piece of this puzzle.

On Monday, September 25, from 12:00 p.m.—2:00 p.m., key proponents of the Waste Not, Orange County program will be coming to Ventura County to share details about their initiative. The informational session will take place in our large conference room at 2240 East Gonzales Road, Suite 200, in Oxnard.

Joining us from Orange County will be Eric Handler, M.D. Health Officer, Orange County, who initiated Waste Not, Orange County and Mike Learakos, Executive Director of Waste Not, Orange County. We are hopeful that you will attend. Please feel free to bring another person from your organization who you believe is knowledgeable or critical to your connection to this initiative. A light lunch will be provided.

— Robert Levin, M.D. Health Officer, Ventura County Public Health

***

Since we were already rescuing food, with Food Share of Ventura County as our best partner, we were a good fit for this new program. Not only were we doing our part to keep food and organic material out of the landfill, we were able to provide millions of pounds of edible food to food-insecure people.

The Environmental Resources Department of the County of Ventura was tasked with the responsibility of educating restaurants about the value of donating safe, unserved food. The excuse for not donating has been the fear of liability. Inroads into the level of cooperation were small. Just this month, a contact was made with Ventura County Medical Center to work on an arrangement for food pickup. We figure most of that food can be enhanced with some salt and butter!

There are state and federal Good Samaritan Laws that protect donors if they hand off the food to a responsible party. The danger for the recipient is to have confidence the food has been kept at safe temperatures during the event. We came close to making a huge mistake one Sunday afternoon. By the time the food returned to Harvard, the smell was bad and we had to discard it.

One of our most memorable rescues was from the Chili Cook Off at Amgen. The caterers prepared food for 10,000 people. We brought home amazing amounts of food, and had to use the refrigerators at the Presbyterian Church. We did that for two years, until I felt the task was too great and risky. We would drop large amounts on our way home to the Salvation Army and the Rescue Mission.

I obtained my ServSafe Certificate early, followed by my Food Manager's Certificate, which keeps our kitchen open and safe.

As we grew our service areas, we included food from Santa Paula and Fillmore school districts, Panera, Starbucks, Pizza Chief and from Palazzio Banquet Center in Santa Paula. It is often enough food for an entire meal or two at Harvard for 50 people. All donated food and rescued food is weighed, examined and sorted. The reporting requirements are extensive and every entity has their own platform. This includes Food Share, which has the responsibility of distributing food from the USDA. Fortunately, our data manager, Mary Ruiz, picks up the food tickets daily and stays on top of reporting. Tom Wilson and Bob Carson were faithful helpers on our Food Share shopping days.

In 2017, my real estate office was still at the 113 N. Mill Street location, so the board decided to include a request for funds to remodel the back of the office to be more suitable for food rescue, storage, distribution and preparation. Susan Kulwiec, board member and talented interior designer, spent dozens of hours re-designing the space. As we were getting ready to pull permits, based on an aggressive and dreamed-up budget of $180,000, that's when Naomi Pitcairn proposed she purchase the old bar in Santa Paula, once known as Buck and Sunny's and the Frontier Club. That's when everything changed.

I decided to move my property management company into the offices of Century 21 Everest and take advantage of that new location at 1498 E. Harvard to consolidate all services—shelter, drop in center, resource center, food pantry and kitchen services. The final move occurred on Dec. 7, 2019.

When the grant application for $180,000 was submitted to the state, the estimated poundage collection was 490 edible tons. Since we were already at 450 tons, we thought it would be easy. Then, someone pointed out to us that it was to be 490 new tons—on top of what we were already doing. No one remembers knowing that when we signed the Memorandum of Understanding (MOU).

When we realized what we needed to do, we signed up for every available store and time slot we could. Managing the inventory was a challenge, because we had to be sure the expiration dates fell after the next available food distribution and pantry event. With the grant money, we were able to buy two refrigerated trucks, but the grant didn't come with a rule book on how to do that. We purchased a beautiful 2021 Hino truck with a refrigerator, but it runs only when the engine is running. It was not a good decision. The 2010 Isuzu had a refrigerator that ran on its own, but it failed shortly after we purchased it. The cost to replace it was $19,000, but we received a discount, making it $16,000. The Gene

Hass Foundation came to the rescue and provided funding. That truck is still operating today.

For many months, SPIRIT held their weekly staff meeting in the back of the refrigerated truck because there was no space at Harvard to have a private meeting.

With the new addition finished, staff now meets in a soundproof room with a smart TV and writing space. They can actually hear each other.

The grant from CalRecyle required that we spend the money and then get reimbursed. There was no way we could buy our trucks under that condition. For the first purchase of the Isuzu, Steve and Kathy Goch fronted the $15,000, which was repaid when SPIRIT was reimbursed. The second truck cost $88,000 and the only way that purchase could happen is if another partner with some serious resources came alongside us. Monica White, the smart and capable CEO of Food Share, put together a plan to loan SPIRIT the purchase cost, and then wait for reimbursement. It worked. The COVID-19 pandemic had just started when the truck was delivered to us. We let Food Share use it for a few weeks to get their food deliveries paced, then the keys were handed off—with proper distancing.

To meet our ambitious tonnage challenge, we picked up food at 9 p.m. from Traders Joes, Albertsons and other stores on Thanksgiving Eve, Thanksgiving Day, Christmas Eve and Christmas Day, New Years Eve and New Year's Day. It was often cold and tiresome. One year, we received a truckload from the Ojai Valley Inn on New Year's Day. We had to rely on volunteers who were willing to give up holidays. It is one thing to collect the food at 9 p.m., and another to resource it and get it put away before signing off for the night. We were often at the site until midnight. I won't say our holidays were spoiled, but they were eventful in a different way. Maria Sanchez was always willing to take on that task and became the house expert on food sourcing.

Included in the grant were funds for kitchen upgrades. As the pieces of the Harvard Shelter operation came together, we were able to upgrade the kitchen at Harvard, and purchase all the necessary equipment to run a first-class kitchen. As a result of our food rescue operations, Harvard serves 175 meals a day with almost a zero food budget. It is amazing what comes from the stores—cases of salt containers, bags of sugar, all kinds of condiments, sauces, meat, potatoes, fresh fruit, pies and pastries, chips and dips, soft drinks, juices and vegetables. We now rescue 171,000 pounds of food each month ... plenty to use and plenty to give away. That amount of food would take up the same space as 1,026 elephants.

The investment CalRecyle made in SPIRIT of Santa Paula has continued to pay dividends. We learned a lot about food rescue and managed to suffer through the most difficult task of reporting our progress to the state and preparing invoices for the county. Thanks to Senator Monique Limon, with support by Assemblymember Bennett, there is talk in Sacramento about forming a state task force to make it easier for nonprofits to request funds and report on expenditures. It takes a full-time person to manage the data and few nonprofits have funding for that task.

We hope there is another program for food rescue, despite the challenges. People have to be fed. It's not fair that food goes to waste or costs so much.

Chapter Thirteen

LUCY AND LEO

Lucy and Leo could be remembered as Santa Paula's most famous couple, not exactly for being Citizens of the Year, but for being unique, challenging, frustrating and often loveable.

Lucy was notable for a couple of reasons. She was featured on *America's Unsolved Mysteries*. At the age of 14, she was found wandering around Port Hueneme. She had no ID and was carrying baby shoes, baby clothes and little else. Lucy was deaf. The theory was that she was flown to the U.S. and separated from the people who brought her. The baby clothes might have been from a baby she delivered. No one ever solved this mystery.

She was taken in by social workers and housed for a while at a group home in the Oxnard area. Lucy was an independent one and decided she would rather make it on her own. She met up with Leo and they traveled together for several years. One day, she had a hint he might have another girlfriend. His demands and his addiction became her burden and she left him behind.

Her street sign language was limited. She could communicate some words, but was rapidly repetitive with the same word, thinking it was appropriate communication. We connected sometime around 2008.

Tri-Counties Regional Services stepped in and was prepared to assist her with housing and services, but Leo was not eligible to join her.

She refused to leave him, so they stayed on the streets. The Greater Los Angeles Agency on Deafness, Inc., (GLAD), in Ventura, knew Lucy and tried to re-engage with her again. Her "street sign language" was so limited, it was nearly impossible to communicate with her.

Leo Zepeda was a different kind of story. He was raised in Santa Paula, and was one of nine children. He was affable, handsome and loved to make friends. He worked for my husband in the early 1990s and was generally late for work, had a black eye or bruises, and often missed a day or two back to back. He would show up on his bicycle with a black eye and various bruises, assuring Howard everything was "just fine."

Lucy and Leo's love story began around 2000. They traveled the streets together and protected each other. They rented a room in a condo complex, but were forced to leave, because they argued a lot. Lucy was loud when she tried to verbalize. I lost a TV in that exit.

They both used drugs and did the typical spiral downward. They lost teeth, lost weight and daily lost something they collected. Lucy was also known for being a fashionista and managed to come up with a new outfit every day, gathered from the various dumpsters around town.

Leo was known for his vast array of items in a Von's shopping cart he called treasures and most of us called junk: a garden hose, a broker mirror, a broken fan, plastic dishes, waste basket and sofa cushions.

Sometime around 2015, Lucy had enough of being bossed around and left for Ventura. I occasionally see her on the streets with a bottle of vodka, and honk and wave, forgetting she cannot hear me.

Lucy Doe was named by the police officer who found her on the streets in Port Hueneme at the age of 14—no ID, no documents and she was deaf. She made her way to Santa Paula and became the companion of Leo Zepeda, a Santa Paula man who became homeless. This is them in about 2010.

Life on the streets is hard. This is a winter day in about 2017 after a night sleeping under the bridge. Her clothes always smelled like smoke and she was always thirsty. Many service providers tried to help her, but their offers did not include Leo, her boyfriend, so she rejected the help.

She has heightened senses and skillfully navigates traffic areas. She rarely honors the crossing lights and thinks nothing of darting into the street. People give her the middle finger salute, honk and yell, without realizing she cannot hear them. I suppose that's a commentary on most of us who are not hearing or seeing, and not recognizing the reality of people's physical challenges.

Leo was lost without her and continued to spiral. He made his home at the entrance of Yanni's Bakery, Big Lots and Von's shopping area. He was fed regularly by strangers and sadly given money, which kept him in his addiction.

He would call me at all hours of the night, asking me to pick him up or bring him food. He would also ask shoppers and shopkeepers to call me. He couldn't remember 911 for emergencies, but he certainly remembered my number.

I had to convince him he could only call me for emergencies during the night—not for food, not for a blanket or a beer. In the early days, he asked for special foods like pastrami sandwiches and pizza with anchovies and olives.

There were regular trips to the hospital, mostly for serious insect bites or a dislocated shoulder. He grew very thin, but maintained a cheerful personality, quickly switching back and forth from laughter to tears. We would sing together all verses of, "A Mighty Fortress is Our God."

His last days were spent sleeping behind Von's amid an array of trash and leftover food. He had been in the hospital for a few days and lived only a few hours on his first day back on the street. He was found dead, likely from an overdose. It was never confirmed, but I believed it to be true. This is common when someone comes clean during a jail sentence or hospital stay. Their body is not used to the typical dose, and as soon as they hit the needle, they die, because their body can't handle it.

I posted Leo's demise on Facebook, and the outpouring of affection and sorrow was overwhelming and comforting to the family. When drug addiction is the center of someone's life, everyone in the circle waits for the news. Sometimes, it comes sooner than later.

Leo was a local favorite and spend his day making friends. Life on the street is hard and he couldn't remember how this injury occured or who did it.

It's odd that outcasts can become folk heroes. No one would take Leo home, but everyone would feed him with the sincere desire to make his life more comfortable.

In reality, it is unwise to take someone into your home whose behavior is unpredictable. In my career, I have only taken someone home once for one night. Looking back, I was lucky nothing bad happened.

Leo's memorial service was held at the Bridge Church and conducted by Pastora Adelita Garza. She spoke about the wonder of his life and the beauty of his personality. I loved her for that. I have been to too many memorials for our street people. I've noticed no one ever mentions how hard they lived and how hard they died.

I wonder if Lucy knows.

Chapter Fourteen

SHELTER PETS

Pets can be an important source of comfort and companionship for homeless individuals.

A homeless person is very protective of their animal and will feed it before they feed themselves. This fuzzy feeling breaks down when the animal gets sick and needs medical attention. They are often dehydrated and eat the opposite of proper food.

They eat what their owners eat and that includes potato chips, meat with salsa, peanuts and popcorn, bread and tortillas, bagels and beer.

When the animal is sick, it suffers and the owner will beg a nonprofit for funds to treat the animal, which can run into the thousands of dollars, and they can rarely be seen the same day. Unfortunately, many homeless shelters do not allow pets, due to various logistical and safety concerns. However, there are some homeless shelters (like Harvard) that have begun to recognize the benefits of allowing pets and have implemented pet-friendly policies.

These shelters may provide accommodations such as pet beds, food and even veterinary care for the pets.

There are also some organizations and programs that specifically focus on providing housing and support for homeless individuals with pets. For example, the nonprofit organization Pets of the Homeless provides food, veterinary care and other services for the pets of homeless individuals across the United States.

Buddy Nation is an organization in Ventura, California, that finds resources for injured animals and provides convalescent care. They are on speed dial for most homeless pet owners in the area. Overall, while there are still many challenges and barriers to providing adequate support for both homeless individuals and their pets, there are efforts being made to address these issues and provide more inclusive and supportive services.

Harvard Shelter has been home to many pets over the years.

The youngest and first was Brownie. He was two months old and a tiny Chihuahua mix. He was black and named by a 5 year-old in the shelter. We were sure that pup knew English. As a baby, he "stayed" when told to stay, jumped up in bed on command and dutifully barked and quieted.

As the family progressed in their efforts to end homelessness, they found a place to live, but could not take the dog. Brownie is currently being fostered, but he never forgot his family.

He knows when they pull in their driveway for a visit, and he cries for a long time when they leave. He is safe for now, but remembers his first love. He's at my house.

Brownie lives with me, because his owners are not allowed to have pets. they could rightly claim "emotional support" but Brownie lives with other dogs and he would not be happy alone. We all do better in community.

Juno was also one of our first shelter pets. He was a little black and white thing and looked like Yoda. Prior to coming to our shelter at the Methodist Church.

Michael was very protective of Juno. We found a playpen, padded it with soft blankets and one morning we found three unbelievably beautiful pups. It was a great distraction for everyone, but there were challenges in making people leave them alone.

We commissioned certain people to monitor them during the day so Michael could work. He cried when I told him it was time for them to leave Juno. We found three wonderful women who gave them great homes, thanks to the oversight of SPARC, the Santa Paula Animal Rescue Center.

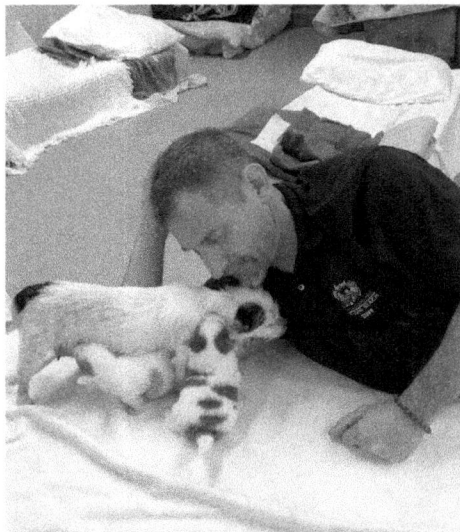

Juno was a unique pup. Michael stayed with family members for a few days and Juno met up with the house Pomeranian. We had to agree they made great puppies. The puppies were born at the shelter and grew to the age of adoption. They were to three different homes and new owners.

Then there was Baby, a cranky and unpredictable pit bull. She lunged at people passing by and growled at anyone who came near. I had a hard conversation with the owner and shared my thoughts about how this dog was going to hold him back, preventing him from finding a job. He didn't care and told me to mind my own business. They want us to provide everything possible, but are convinced what happens in the shelter that affects their future is none of our business.

Then there was Candy, the poodle princess, owned by a 45-year-old man, who left his wife and took the dog. She was everyone's favorite and wandered from bed to bed, asking for comfort and of course food. Everyone was quick to respond with both.

Candy was owned by Martin's wife. When they separated, Martin took the pup. Candy was a nervous guest and was sent back and forth between her owners. She was a favorite in the room.

Snoopy lived at the riverbed and had the run of open spaces. His owner was an addict. One Sunday night at about 9 p.m., Snoopy was riding in the basket of his owner's bicycle and he bounced out. His foot was caught in the spokes and his pad was torn off. Milo brought Snoopy to Harvard and begged for help. I called the backline at SPARC and the manager told me to take him to Horizon's Vet Emergency Clinic, in Ventura.

The fee was $5,000 to repair the damage. No one had a budget for anything close to that. SPARC stepped in and said they would pay the bill, but Milo had to agree to have the dog neutered. He refused.

The next day Milo was arrested and went to jail for several days. Meanwhile, the dog was going untreated and infection set in. SPARC rules are that if the dog is not claimed in five days, it can be adopted. I told them I would take the dog after he was repaired and neutered. By then, the infection was severe and on that Friday, Snoopy's leg was amputated.

I adopted Snoopy and let him stay at Harvard. Todd took charge of Snoopy, whose name was changed to Harvey. (Harvard—Harvey). He kept Harvey leashed and the dog developed a bad habit of nipping at people when they walked by his bed.

One feisty woman claimed Harvey bit her, so I knew he had to leave Harvard. He lives at my house now, and he and Brownie are now like caballeros. Harvey visited Harvard once a week and would run to Todd's bed as soon as he arrived.

Snoopy's first owner died of an overdose and Todd later died from a heart attack while visiting friends at the river bed.

Rusty was the house sweetheart. A little terrier-sized dog with red hair. He didn't need a leash, because he was attentive to his owner and stayed close. The kids in the shelter would fuss over who Rusty would sleep with at night. When it came time for Matt to leave Harvard, we were happy for Matt, and we cried about Rusty.

Now there is Luna. She is a large dachshund type and very obedient. Her owner is Cristina, and she gets great care. One night at house meeting, we discovered the kids had been teasing Luna through the cage. It was an ugly confrontation between parents who think, "kids are just being kids," and the protective dog owner. I voted on the side of Luna.

Harvard Shelter is scored on three of many things. One is to prevent homelessness. The second is to move people from the shelter into permanent supportive housing. The third one got us a ding, because our case management services failed—sort of.

Oreo, the black and white cat, was born at Harvard Shelter. After his litter mate was killed on Harvard Boulevard, we found permanent supportive housing with a nice lady about two miles from Harvard. She had a friendly cat, who wanted a roommate. So, Oreo left on good terms and into a great placement. Sadly, Oreo went missing for three weeks and we regretted making him move.

One morning, we were overjoyed to learn Oreo was at Harvard, asking Melinda to feed him. I decided he will stay with us as "mental health support," so there will be no more dings. Welcome home, Oreo. Shelter is as Shelter does.

There is a hay barn near Harvard Shelter and we have had a number of stray and feral cats live among us. Oreo is on the right and we were able to get him neutered and vaccinated. He now has his own bed and will stay with us.

What we have learned about humanity, and the love of their pets is heartwarming. Comfort and affection goes both ways and there is a sadness and void when that comes to an end. The jury is still debating how to evaluate that love against the unintentional neglect of basic veterinary care.

Here are just a few photos of our beloved shelter pets over the years:

Chase came from a family with six kids and lived a frantic life. he was so attached to all of them. He came to live with me for a while. Mama was committed to finding permanent housing and she did. A thoughtful owner agreed to let Chase go home.

Homelessness took a heavy toll on Clyde. He lived with his family including three children. His trauma came from somewhere before he arrived at Harvard. He was unpredictable, cranky and easily provoked to bites. We sheltered him, no matter what, on the condition he stay on a leash and with the family.

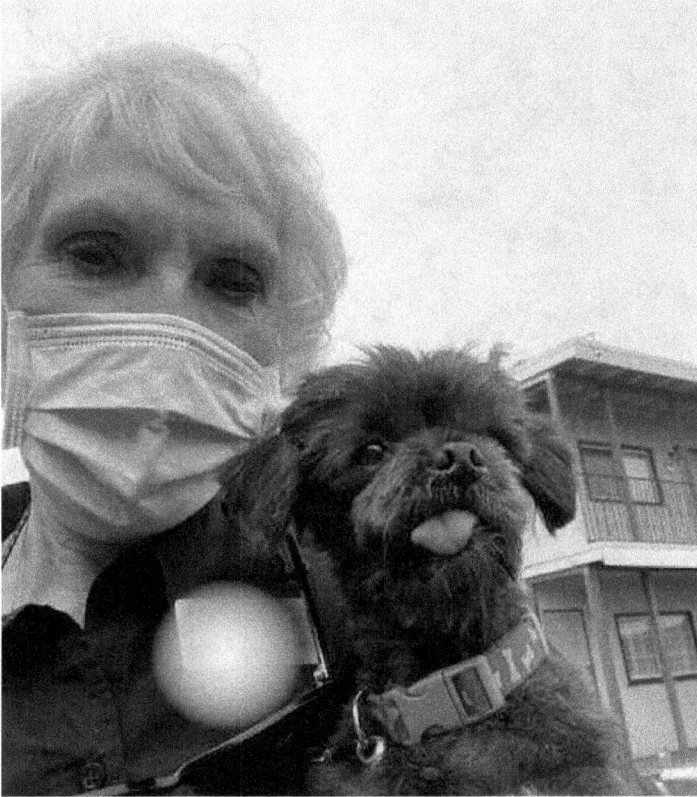

One day a Ventura police officer called and asked if we would help a woman who had just been put out of a motel. She was in a wheel chair and had this little dog named Leo. He had an extreme underbite and had to have special food. We had to work with a variety of agencies to get Clara what she needed. After a much needed surgery, she spent months in skilled nursery. Leo lives with a family member.

Roxie was a house favorite and loved everyone. He was very loyal to his owners but would let anyone love on him. He was particularly fond of Leanna, our shelter assistant. When a guest leaves us, we are equally sad to say goodbye to their pets.

Shorty Vaughn was a unique one. He was part Chihuahua and something else. His owner was Sherry Vaughn and lived at my office for many months until she moved to Lancaster after her parents died. One day when Shorty was sick, a good citizen called me from the fountain on Main Street asking me to do something. I picked up Sherry and Shorty and drove them to a vet's office. Shorty died in her arms on the way. He is buried in my backyard.

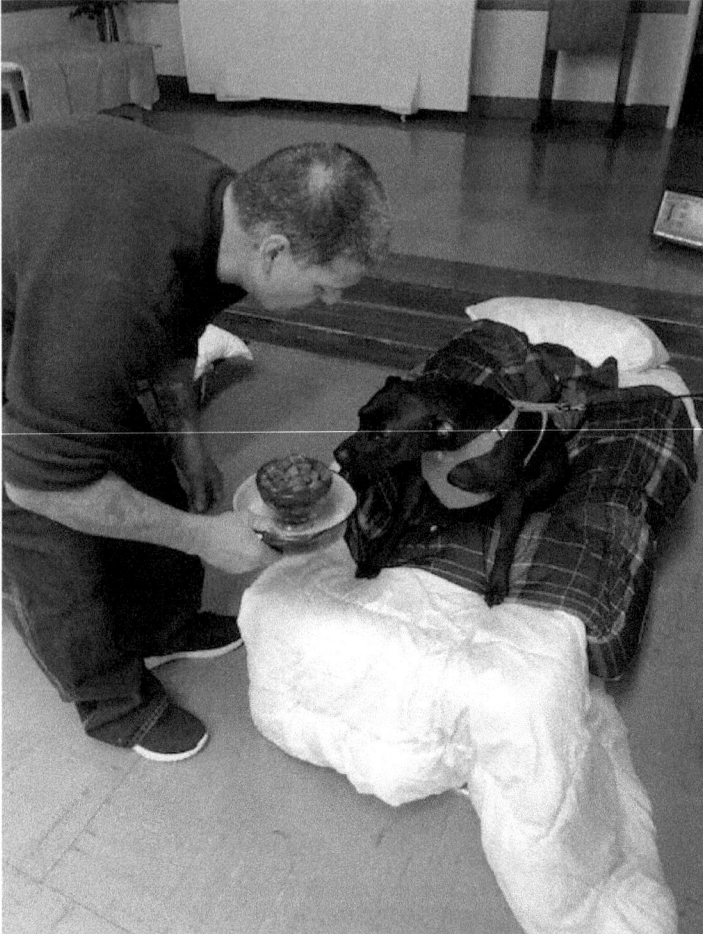

Baby was the beloved dog of Eric. Baby was very attached to Eric and not a friendly pup. He was jumpy, edgy and snappy. Despite our many encouragements for Eric to rehome the dog so he could get a job, he refused to part with her. Experts told us the dog would be easy to place. Eric left the shelter and we heard some time later Baby had died. I wondered how Eric managed that loss.

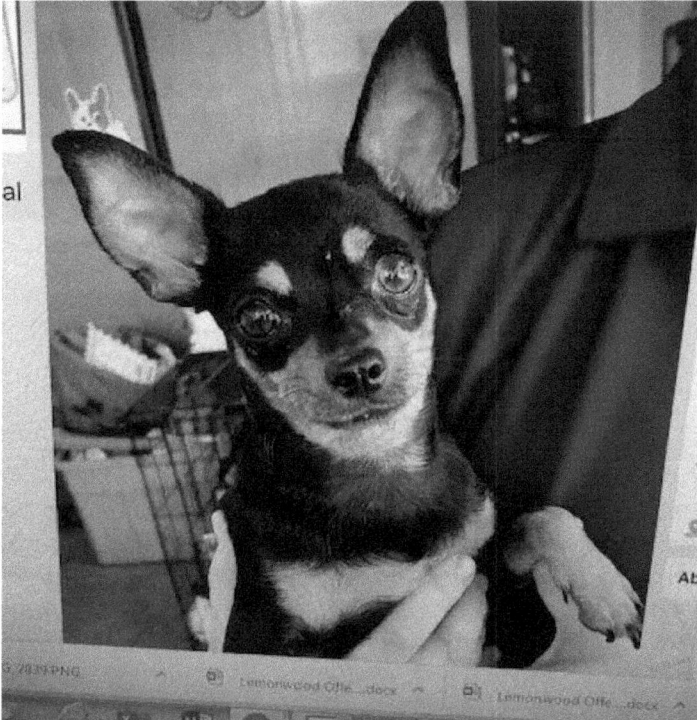

Picasso was the most popular dog with big ears and a big heart. He lived with Jack in our first shelter, in Jack's trucks for months and odd places for people to live. He was a devoted little dog who loved to be hugged and would sit in your lap for hours. One day, Picasso got scared during a traffic incident. When Jack pulled over, Picasso jumped out and ran without caution. He was hit by a car and died. Jack was inconsolable and so were we.

These two buddies, Slash and Axel, belonged to a man experiencing homelessness. Buddy Nation volunteers did their best to help the owner with the dogs' needs. All was good until it wasn't. The owner suffered from mental health challenges and often put the dogs in danger. When police were called, the dogs knew safety had arrived and they would jump into the police car and hang out until it was time to travel to the shelter.

Chapter Fifteen

POLICE PROBLEMS AND PERSONALITIES

Not all first responders share our affection for people who are experiencing homelessness. While I debated the risk of including this chapter, I feel it is important to show the disparity in training and attitudes among some officers. Much of it has to do with the leader of the department—generally true of any organization.

I'm sure the officer involved in this controversy has her own view of what happened. She is welcome to tell her story anywhere and to whomever she likes. This is ours. I will not use her name. She knows who she is.

We experienced a situation where an officer issued a biased and unfair citation against one of our managers, Sabriana. Some police officers in town remember when Sabriana's family was homeless and they took occasions to be critical and unkind. However, Sabriana and Nomi succeeded in overcoming extremely difficult circumstances that have overwhelmed many others. I devote an entire chapter to their story later in the book, which makes what happened to Sabriana all the more exasperating.

It was a rainy, windy and cold morning at Harvard Shelter. Our street clients were beginning to arrive for hot coffee. We moved the serving tables just inside the shelter, so staff and guests could have some moments of warmth.

We seldom talk about our shelter being a dangerous place, because it isn't. Realistically, based on what kind of night our street people have, the day can range from pleasant and happy to noisy and scary. Instincts tell most of us to respond to danger, especially when in charge of the environment.

On Thursday, Jan. 26, 2023, Hugo arrived for coffee. He was drunk, loud, shouting and demanding. An intoxicated individual, who is belligerent and boisterous, should not be in the building. However, it was only to pick up his breakfast and leave. The shelter supervisor that morning was Sabriana. She knew what to do. Four-year-old Mia was nearby, watching how adults react to dangerous situations.

Sabriana took Hugo by the arm and guided him to the door, while Maria called 911, using the words, "violent, aggressive and possibly dangerous." Hugo was still protesting, but cooperating. When Sabriana got him on the other side of the doors, he tried to open them, but Sabriana held them shut.

Fifteen minutes later, the officer arrived with her partner. She had her cop face on and asked what happened. Sabriana told the story of what happened, and the officer began to interrogate Hugo, asking if Sabriana touched him. Three times she asked if he wanted to press charges against Sabriana for battery. He finally said yes.

She turned to Sabriana, said she was under arrest and read her rights.

There are many troubling things about this situation.

Immediate action was needed by someone to remove the unruly and intoxicated Hugo from the building. Staff member Maria Aguirre called 911 immediately and used the right words.

The officer was more concerned about Hugo than she was about the staff member who professionally, carefully and safely removed him from the building before she arrived.

At no time did the officer inquire about the safety or well-being of Sabriana, who de-escalated the situation. At no time did she ask if she was touched, pushed or hurt.

Everyone was stunned when the officer told Sabriana she was being cited for misdemeanor battery. Three complaints were filed against this officer. We asked for an apology and for her to un-arrest Sabriana.

We carry no weapons, pepper spray, tasers or clubs. We need support in the exercise of our duties. We called 911 and reported a dangerous situation. No one came for 15 minutes. In that time, a lot of people could have been hurt and damage done if Sabriana had not stepped in.

When the Alhambra gunman was disarmed by a bystander at the Lai Lai Ballroom, that 26-year-old was applauded as a hero. Sabriana acted in the same way, without regard for her own safety, but was penalized.

Our video of the incident is very clear, showing Sabriana's skillful removal of Hugo Chavez from the shelter and de-escalating, if not defusing, his intrusion. The officer refused to look at the video, which clearly would have influenced her attitude and actions.

Many other officers in our small department would have handled this differently. We believe the officer has a personal bias toward homeless people in general, and the people who serve them. That attitude over-rode her ability to make a reasonable judgment.

I recognize the officer's responsibility to write a citation in some situations, but this was prompted by her poking Hugo about pressing charges. The same care should have been extended to Sabriana. This officer failed to protect all members of the public equally and chose to side with the perpetrator.

Sabriana deserves an apology and needs to be un-arrested. Fortunately, the district attorney agrees with us and nothing will be filed, but we had many nervous moments. While no charges were filed, the DA reserved the right to look at this again, under any new circumstances.

This officer needs sensitivity training and education on the need to practice trauma-informed care in the exercise of her duties. She also needs to prevent personal bias from interfering with her ability to be fair.

Many of our officers view us as partners in dealing with this particular segment of our community, and we enjoy back and forth support. That was a dark day for us, and the staff is fearful about what will happen the next time this officer arrives. We are also unclear about what measures we should take to protect the environment, in light of similar potential danger. When the third complaint was delivered to the station, the officer of the day chided the member of the public, asking if one wasn't enough.

Santa Paula's new interim chief of police is Donald Aguilar. He met with SPIRIT board members and staff to help us understand what happened and what to do next time. We appreciated what he tried to do, but everyone left the meeting not knowing exactly what to do next time.

Fortunately, that officer has been assigned to another unit and won't be visiting Harvard again in an enforcement capacity. Officer Dan Gosselin is assigned to us. He's a good ally and helps us make good decisions while he protects everyone. He joins us for weekly staff meetings, to gain insight on how well we prepare for our work and to learn how he can help us do our jobs safely.

Chapter Sixteen

HOW MANY TIMES CAN YOU GET ARRESTED?

It was May 30, 2018, when it happened again. Rey was belligerent, half-dressed and wandering the streets talking to himself. He was arrested a week prior. That makes 15 times since 2015 and many of these were in the last few months. What to do?

Rey came to Many Meals for food and to intimidate. This time he was waving a baseball bat, shouting and scaring people. The previous Sunday, he accepted an invitation to attend church. When I arrived at 9:30 a.m., he was sitting on the front wall shaving. This is like a foreign land to members of this church, whose history is founded in the members of influence and wealth.

Police can do nothing other than arrest Rey, until he is declared "gravely disabled." It won't be soon. Rey is very resourceful, having lived on the streets for several years. His brother, Leo, was also on the streets until he died, as was a brother before him, who died while incarcerated in the Todd Road jail. What is the common thread?

The last arrest was when Rey set Chase Bank on fire. He spent two years in jail, and when released, he came to Harvard Shelter. His attentive sister, Dora, visited him regularly and helped with his medication prescribed by Behavioral Health. Rey would have been happy to stay at Harvard for the rest of his life. We were leery about bringing him to

Harvard, but he begged for a chance. After two years, he left us for a group home and is doing well.

Sometimes, the change comes when the perpetrator gets too old to participate. Rey was 72 years old when he left us. He didn't have the energy to do much more than sleep, eat and smoke.

Without case management, people languish and stay in their rut. One homeless man in another part of the County visited the emergency room 152 times last year. Carol died in January and was at the Santa Paula hospital ER no less than an estimated 30 times. I took her on numerous occasions and she was transported by medical professionals many more times. The nurses at Santa Paula Hospital were often impatient with her. She had raw and gaping wounds on her legs and was injecting heroin into them. Despite her denials, everyone knew it was true.

Magda was arrested for throwing a rock through a car window. She'll be out soon. And the cycle begins again. She is homeless half of the time, couch surfing here and there, panhandling and stealing.

Lisa was arrested for being under the influence ... again. This is at least arrest number 20.

The Friday One Stop program, sponsored by Ventura County's Continuum of Care and supervised by James Boyd, made many inroads into helping our people find their way. County professionals were on hand to provide the necessary links to services.

A hot shower is everything to a person on the streets. Some are lazy, however, and come by the Drop In Center at my office for a breakfast snack and then decide to forego the shower, because they don't like to wait in line. We started a laundry program on Friday mornings, supervised by Carolyn Tulberg.

The idea was to wash their clothes so they would have clean clothes to wear after their shower and appointment at One Stop. We had to stop the program after five years, because of many abuses. They would bring the clothing of their friends. People who were housed would pretend to be homeless. People would arrive at the laundry and tie up all the machines waiting for Carolyn, which prevented the regular customers from using the equipment.

James Boyd, from the Whole Person Care program, agreed we will close the Drop In Center at my office on Friday mornings, and instead serve a light breakfast at One Stop, stationed at El Buen Pastor Methodist Church, so there would be no excuse for missing this important engagement.

At One Stop, they see a doctor or a nurse, get assistance with their MediCal and other benefits, including Pathways to Home, and get entry into the Homeless Management Information System. The shower pod at One Stop was provided by CarePodz.

Through that program, four of our people have found rentals—one in Camarillo, one in Ventura and two seniors right here in town. While they prefer to stay in Santa Paula, it's likely a good idea for them to relocate, so they can make new friends and opportunities, while avoiding old influences.

There are many reasons for homelessness, besides alcohol and drug abuse. Below are some examples.

A woman with three children had her water turned off, because her family stopped helping with the monthly payments. There is a backstory to this, but while the property was posted with a disconnect notice, the water remained on. She thought the bill had been paid. She came in on a recent Friday with a water bill of over $1,000. Someone called Child Protective Services and reported her for living in a home with children with no water, making the dwelling uninhabitable. Thanks to Father Charles, at Our Lady of Guadalupe Church, we raised the money to get the water back on.

Another single mother with six children, attending school to become an X-ray technician, couldn't start her car on a recent Friday. We had it tuned up as someone suggested: $184. No luck. We put in a new starter: $139. No luck. Finally, we put in a new battery and still no luck: $179. Someone suggested a new ignition, which apparently leads to other things and we realized the 1999 car isn't worth fixing.

Her children attend school in another city for several reasons, and she has to transport them on her way to school/work.

Another woman working closely with the county to get housing discovered her "free government phone" died. There go her contacts and her appointments. She has no way of communicating with the outside world that can rescue her. So, we got her a new phone, which also means a new phone number.

The absence of money is one thing; the absence of resources to solve problems is another. Many Meals continued to be the link to fragile people. A woman came in recently, who was so anxious to be around people, she almost fainted.

Fortunately, Ted Perez from Behavioral Health stopped by after work and recognized what was going on. He reached out to her and was able to make an appointment right away and they connected again. She came to our food pantry on a recent Saturday and she called to see if anyone was able to give her $20, so she could pay someone to bring her into town to get food.

The Bible talks a lot about money and how wonderful it is to give it. It is the love of money that traps us, but I have noticed many are trapped, due to its absence and scarcity. One seemingly small event can turn a family upside down and jeopardize their ability to pay rent, leading to eventual homelessness.

We can't buy batteries for every car or pay everyone's water bills. It seems we are presented with one or two at a time who we can help, and with some of the angels who hang out with us, we make a difference. Susan Kulwiec, Jill Wallerstedt and I regularly wrote grants to find funds to help stabilize our families and be the safety net they need to get through a day. I just pray their kids grow up to be successful and able to support their parents in later years, as a "thank you" for the hard work done in these years.

Our work is more than just with those finding shelter in the streets. It extends to the least powerful and most vulnerable in our community in the form of prevention.

The City Council established an Ad Hoc Committee to study and work on the issues of homelessness. The first members were Jenny Crosswhite and John Procter, two fresh faces looking at the problems and opportunities, and willing to engage the locals on what is being done and must be done. It has morphed into today's Task Force on Homelessness. Members now include the Police Commander Eric Starna, Officer Dan Gosselin, Community Development Director James Mason, Council members Pedro Chavez and Carlos Juarez, Nomi Marrufo, Sabriana Marrufo and myself as director. It's a new day.

The new partnership with the city puts all conversations and interactions at a new level of communication and cooperation.

However, there is another side to this work that hurts. One of the men who lives on the streets as a result of alcohol addiction has been asking for another phone. He is one who misses appointments, won't attend the One Stop service center, consistently asks for bus fare so he can visit people in Ventura and is taking his medication with alcohol. He makes promises he doesn't keep and sleeps at a local church. He called from the Job and Career Center and challenged me about when I was going to get him his new phone. I told him I wanted him to use some of his monthly check to get one. He flared back stating, "My talk was cheap" and he had no use for me. He called the next day to ask about his new phone. It's all a test, you know. Will I be there for them, no matter what, or not?

Many of those on the street think little of being arrested. It's no big deal. They talk about "three hots and a cot" as though the arrest is worth it. It's one of the cycles that has to be intercepted. Change will come when they are sufficiently tired. Until then, we keep the doors open and guard our hearts.

Chapter Seventeen

DANGEROUS FRIENDS

In addition to our clients who live in the shelter, we also have a street outreach program outside the building, where people who are living on the streets can come for a meal or other help. Many of them want to sabotage our work, because their behavior has made them not eligible to come into the shelter. Even a few police officers comment that, "Kay has her favorites."

Rather than hold people accountable for their behavior that either disqualified them from shelter life or their refusal to come in when a bed is available, these officers court the favor of those on the streets, by blaming me or our manager for them remaining unsheltered. Accountability seems to get misappropriated at every level of society.

There's a sage story about a pot of frogs. They learn that the way to climb out of the pot is to climb over others and push them to the bottom. It's the way they elevate themselves. In the spring of 2023, there were two people who frequented the shelter who I considered to be dangerous: Marsha and a 15-year-old named Julie.

Marsha was a transgender female with an unpredictable personality. We honored her by using her pronoun "she." She loved to stir up trouble. She incited people to be mad at me. She accused our staff of stealing from her, then told everyone in the community about it. But I'm the one she called when her battery was dead, or she ran out of gas on the freeway or needed to cash a check from a relative.

Marsha was a popular hairdresser in Santa Paula, until drugs became more attractive. I have a series of pictures of Marsha over the last 12 years. If you saw the first one and the last one, you would not know it was the same person. She has caused us so much grief. She threatened to sue one of my staff members, who she claims stole money from her. Then she called her family members and got them mad at us. It goes on. However, due to diligent and thoughtful case management, Marsha was moved to a motel in Ventura, instead of on the streets or in the back of a van.

I do call her a "friend," because she sidles up to us. We know it's our calling to do what we can to help. I can't recall how many times I have rescued her in her vehicle. She was living in a van and couldn't get it started one Saturday evening. She was parked in the wrong place and subject to being towed. It was 7 p.m. on a Saturday night and I went to the parts store, bought a battery and had it changed out. The next day, the van got towed by the police department, because it wasn't registered.

One time, it was my turn to be mad. She ran out of gas on the highway, between exits about five miles apart. I bought gas, went all the way down to the far freeway exit, turned around and pulled up behind her. Another car was there. I said, "Marsha, I thought you needed gasoline?" She said, "I do. My aunt got here first, but I'll take yours, too." She put me in a dangerous situation on a busy highway to put gas in her car, which she really didn't need to get where she wanted to go. She was staying in Oxnard and would figure out how to get to Santa Paula, but never had enough money to get back home.

She rarely thought of others first. When she was very sick, she wanted us to transport her in our staff car. She refused to go with a 911 first responder, because she said they ask too many questions.

Marsha often showed up at the shelter agitated. One day, she wanted her mail, so Sabriana gave it to her and Marsha accused her of opening it. Sabriana told her she would not retrieve her mail again and she needed to leave the property. Marsha charged at Sabriana, screaming, calling her a prostitute, and threatened to have people come and rough her up. Sabriana closed the fence and called the police department, canceling the call after Marsha left.

There have been several altercations when Marsha threw food or detergent at staff members. She accused Jill, her case worker, of stealing her money after Jill paid for her to have a campsite over a weekend. The ranger called and complained about how the campsite was left. Jill cleaned up the campsite where Marsha had peed and pooped on her clothes and the tent. It hurts when people you love and help turn on you.

Thanks to good case management, Jill Wallerstedt, the Street Outreach Case Manager, was able to get Marsha into Project RoomKey through the Continuum of Care. It meant Marsha was 15 miles from the center of activity in Santa Paula and she suffered from the isolation. We learned she managed to get a friend assigned to her personal care through In Home Services and took him into the motel room.

Marsha soon got a puppy, and because of no training, the puppy did what puppies do. Marsha would leave the dog alone in the motel room, barking for hours. One day, Marsha called and yelled at me, Jill and Sabriana. She wanted us to drive to Ventura and take her to the hospital. There is liability in taking someone in a vehicle, so we told her to call 911, which she did.

Jill picked up the dog from the motel room and kept it for a few days. Marsha knew she had the dog, but reported the dog stolen and caused Jill so much heartache.

Marsha was released from the hospital, and Jill returned the dog to her. Not long after, Marsha went back to the hospital and died a few days later, in June 2023. We never knew what happened to the little dog after that.

The Havoc of a 15-Year-Old

Julie came to Harvard Shelter as what we call an "unescorted youth." She was a 15-year-old girl, who was going on 30—manipulative and scary in the way she reacted to people.

She wanted to stay in the shelter, but I couldn't take her, because she was a minor. I found her mother's phone number and spoke to her. I discovered the mother had moved from Santa Paula to Oregon. She told me, "Kay, I know who you are. Julie doesn't want to come to Oregon with me, but I had to move. And her dad lives in Bakersfield. If you don't mind, she can stay with you if you just keep her safe. That's okay with me."

I called Child Protective Services and told them I had a 15-year-old unescorted minor in the shelter and her mother had just given me permission to let her stay here. I asked what to do about that? They said, "Kay, we know you and you've had kids there before. If you're willing, go ahead and keep her safe. But, she has to be in school." It seemed like a good idea at the time, but Julie was her own kind of trouble.

I eventually found her grandmother in Camarillo, 25 miles away. Julie had been living with her, but she couldn't handle her. So, a 15-year-old ends up on the streets, because everyone moves away.

Julie learned how to live her life in a gang atmosphere with a gang mentality. Gang members don't care who they hurt or what consequences they have to face. They don't care about what happens to them tomorrow. They live for today, because that's all they believe they have.

It worked out fine for a couple of days. Then, I found out Jay was her boyfriend and they were messing around before she came in. It got worse. She was belligerent, wouldn't follow rules, wouldn't come in on time, sign in or out, and wouldn't do chores. Hateful, terrible things were always coming out of her mouth. One day, she called the police and filed charges against Jay for having sex with a minor. He was terrified of going to prison.

Soon, Julie began to tease Jay's buddy, John (also a guest at Harvard), which created problems between the two young men. Jay obtained a restraining order against her to keep her away from him. She followed him to the laundromat and to the store, and made it appear that he was trying to connect with her.

When John also started messing around with this girl, I decided she could not stay at Harvard and called the police. They came to Harvard and they called her father in Bakersfield. He drove to Santa Paula with the intention to "kidnap" her—put her in the car and drive her home. But she refused to get in the car with him. We took her inside to have lunch and she told her father to F-off. She was going to stay in Santa Paula and "do it her way." I had to send her out onto the streets. Part of me wondered how you do that to a 15-year-old girl? But she was not a 15-year-old girl. She was a 15-year-old terrorist, who had somehow gotten through life by learning early on how to be in charge of everybody else's.

It's admirable to go the distance with someone who needs everything you have to give. But, you can derail the organization. Even now, I don't know where she is living. However, I do know she is in Santa Paula. She goes to school when she feels like it—or not. The police have reached a point where they ignore her, because there's no way to deal with her. No foster person would ever take her in, knowing her background. So, a 15-year-old girl lives like that and it's hard to imagine what her future holds.

Jay awaits trial and whether or not he can defend himself against the sex charges. He sees her on the side, but denies it. Then, she calls the police and tells them she's been with him, which brings the law into the mix—again.

This 15-year-old is running the show. Her parents can't handle her. I'm sure they tried and gave up. Her mother may have moved to Oregon to get her away from Santa Paula, but Julie just refused to go. There's a new husband in the mother's life, who likely has given up as well. I had to make her leave Harvard and that was a terrible day.

She's not alone. I think there are millions of kids who have had to grow up like this. They figure out how to manage the streets, so they can do exactly what they want to do—hustle where they want to—consequences be damned. It's a sad situation with a bad outcome.

Chapter Eighteen

GENERATIONAL POVERTY

The complex phenomenon of generational poverty exposes a distressing reality, where economic hardship is passed down from one generation to the next, creating a cycle that seems almost inescapable. Within this cycle, homelessness becomes the stark consequence that demands our attention, empathy and collective action.

It's easy to talk about "the poor" or "the homeless" as broad categories, often overlooking the humanity within these communities. Labels can inadvertently reduce people to mere statistics. By acknowledging the uniqueness of each person's experiences, we can foster a deeper understanding of the multifaceted challenges they face and work toward solutions that address their needs. One of these individuals is Vero.

It was about 2009 when I first met her. She was a regular at Many Meals, and it was in the early days when I thought simple things could solve what I saw as big problems.

Vero had lost many of her teeth and the rest showed a lack of any recent attempt to brush them. On one particular Wednesday, I brought a toothbrush and toothpaste for Vero at Many Meals and gently suggested that I wanted her to be healthy.

She explained why she doesn't brush her teeth. She's too busy and has things to do.

Vero has two daughters, a son, and an off relationship with their father. I would visit Vero at their apartment, where I noticed an abandoned vehicle, trash and many people from the streets hanging out. I sensed then she was not far from an eviction. Landlords don't like those things.

Sadly, within 90 days, she had been evicted. She managed to find a smaller place to live, but lost it as well.

She began living on the streets and progressed from smoking pot to becoming an active meth user. Her health deteriorated, and the signs of street life were taking their toll.

Most people don't realize the consequences of living life without teeth to properly chew food, and the inability to eat many of the proper foods such as meat, fruit, nuts, cereals and vegetables. Everything has to be soft.

Vero acquired two shopping carts and managed to keep them stuffed with essential items for street life—trash bags, water, lotion, cigarettes, cardboard and treasures she deemed necessary. A woman on the streets, particularly at night, is an invitation to tragedy.

Her husband became a guest at Harvard Shelter and had his own health and drug problems. Soon, their son joined him. He wanted to be like the other kids in high school, so we made arrangements for him to join the football team. Donors paid for his equipment, but it soon became impossible for him to make practice and he decided it was too hard to try.

He, too, became a guest at Harvard at the age of 23. He and his dad struggled with simple things, such as making their beds, staying out of the kitchen, not using the F-word and showering daily.

Dad managed to get a job at a local business. He argued with his boss and was fired after five days. He didn't care, he said.

His friend advocated for his boss to hire him, but his attitude again got in the way and he was fired. He didn't care, he said.

It wasn't long before both dad and son were permanently dismissed from Harvard.

Allowing people to skate on following basic rules is a hazard in the house.

Margaret is one of Vero's daughters with a teenage son. They're living in her car. Their daughter Audrey is in a mixed race marriage. They've had their share of problems, which I don't want to cite here. They eventually moved to another city, where housing is more affordable.

Actually, moving away from family was likely a good idea. Today, we do not know where father and son are living. We see Vero in the street sometimes, packing her stuff. She has become sullen and distant.

The entire family stayed at our winter shelters in the early days. Three generations under one roof in a church building. It was raining outside. Because a son-in-law had a criminal record, he was not allowed to stay with his family. He would stay outside the doors, even when it was raining—drunk.

It's been 13 years since those days. Nothing is better, and many things are worse. The kids are older and seem to be walking on the only path they have known.

Three generations lost, stuck and hopeless. At least for now.

Sadly, this is a photo of the very thing that irritates communities. Vero is a mom of three children, two of which are also experiencing homelessness. The father finally escaped the scene and went to live with family members in another state. Homelessness is messy. And, nearby restrooms are locked at night.

Chapter Nineteen

THE LUIS AND BESSIE STORY

Most of us who live privileged lives, or at least have a support system to bolster us through hard times, cannot imagine how the chronically and generationally impoverished live. Bessie and Luis are prime examples of people who are just trying to survive the only way they know how. This is their story.

They were introduced to SPIRIT of Santa Paula sometime in 2015, when they volunteered at our Many Meals project. Their story is one of despair and hopelessness, punctuated by spots of success, which took them from homeless to home. Even so, they struggle with generational poverty and reliance on government funding for the most basic of needs. That will be their lot for the rest of their lives.

They met in the Spring of 2004 at Manny's Garage. Luis was working at Jonesy's Liquor. After chatting for a while, Bessie agreed to meet Luis at 11 p.m. when he finished his shift.

She was married at the time, but they had a fight and she left her husband. Luis was staying at Santa Paula Inn, so he picked up a six pack and they met at his room. Bessie confessed to Luis about how her husband treated her and that he was staying at the Harvard Motel (no relation to Harvard Shelter). The next day, Luis learned Bessie and her husband fought all the time and had separated three or four times.

Luis was given an opportunity to run a local smoke shop and he moved to Harvard Motel, where he, again, met up with Bessie. She used to go to work with him. One night, Luis got sick and went to the emergency room in Ventura, where he learned he needed open heart surgery. They moved together to a motel in Ventura where, in preparation for surgery, where they got very drunk.

After the surgery, Bessie stayed in the hospital with Luis for a week. When they left the hospital, they moved in with Luis's brother. Soon after that, Bessie and her husband got back together and began living in his van.

One night, Luis and his brother got into a fight and Luis was forced to move. He retrieved his medicine and went to the railroad tracks to sleep. He was on the street for two days when Bessie called him to say she and her husband had been fighting and they were at McDonald's. Luis went there, walked up to the group and told Bessie, "Let's go. You're going with me."

It wasn't long before Luis lost his job. He and Bessie left Ventura and came back to Santa Paula, where they lived on the street. They stayed in the barranca—a deep ravine—and made it their home with lots of spiders, insects and snakes. They would awaken at 6 a.m. and scavenge for cans to recycle and sell, then buy beer. They made friends with other homeless people in the area. Bessie's husband would follow them in his van, until he eventually joined them and bought everyone beer.

One of the men had an apartment, and one rainy afternoon he asked Bessie and Luis to stay with him and be his caretaker. He had dialysis treatment three times a week. After three months, he made them leave and they went back to the barranca, which was their home for two years.

Luis had a brother and two sisters, who knew where they were staying and how they lived, but didn't help them. Sometimes, they went hungry. They would go behind Von's or the Chinese place, where they throw the food away, but they put it on plates and would cover it for homeless and hungry people to retrieve. The food was cold, but tasty. Sometimes, they went behind the theater, where they put all the leftover popcorn in big bags. It was not unusual for that to be all they ate in a day.

One August, they were visiting Bessie's husband, when Luis had a stroke and his left side was paralyzed. He was restricted to a wheelchair and Bessie pushed him all over town for a week. He was taking blood thinners with his beer and he had a seizure. Then there were a few more seizures, but Bessie never left his side.

Bessie received $800 in Social Security, which they spent on beer and his cigarettes. One New Year's, they got a room at the Harvard Motel, where he fell and broke the toilet. Fortunately, he was intoxicated enough that he was not injured.

Luis's older sister helped him apply for Social Security and was designated his payee. One day, his sister said her landlord agreed to allow Luis to move in, but not Bessie. He wouldn't leave Bessie, so his sister helped them get an apartment behind Circle K.

Luis's brother moved in with them, because he and his wife had a fight and she threw him out. After about two weeks, his wife started visiting him. One Halloween night, his brother's wife arrived drunk. They had a fight and she was sent to the hospital. Everyone in Luis's family was an alcoholic, except his mom.

As time passed, Luis's sister started complaining that the water bill was too high and they were buying too many groceries. Luis's sister told them it would be better if they moved. They moved to Santa Ana Street and she started taking care of Bessie's money, too. Every week, Luis's sister had new clothes, but not them.

They found an apartment on Ventura Street and Luis told his sister they wanted to move. She convinced them to move in with her and rent a room for only $450 dollars a month.

It turned out to be a mistake. They stayed in their room all the time and only went downstairs to eat. His sister asked them to help with the water bill. They gave her $150 a month for water, and when the sister left every weekend, they cleaned.

Luis and Bessie each received $150 for food stamps. His sister and his niece would go grocery shopping with their food stamps, but she was supposed to take them grocery shopping, so they could use their own stamps. His sister would hide their food and use Luis's food first. On the weekend, she'd cook Luis's meat and invite the family and her boyfriend for dinner. After they got done eating, they'd call Luis and Bessie downstairs to eat the leftovers. Then, everyone would start drinking.

Luis talked to his doctor about his sister being the payee. When the doctor said he was "good," he took over his own and Bessie's money. A month later, they moved into their own apartment.

When Luis told his sister he was taking over his own money, she told him they were on their own and she would no longer help. She stopped talking to them, and that was 13 years ago.

When Bessie and Luis moved into their apartment, Bessie was still married and wanted to get a divorce. They went to the hall of justice to get the papers, and four months later, she was divorced. In 2023, they decided to marry on July 15. It was to be a wedding in the park, where the First Presbyterian Church holds a Sunday service.

Bessie met Bill Fowlie, a local handyman, retired CPA and real estate broker. Bill had a food pantry at his church and Bessie started volunteering. Luis joined her and they began to make friends.

In 2014, when Bessie's mom died, the family sold her house and Bessie got $5,000, so they bought a car, a Ford Blazer. It turned out to be a lemon. They put water in it every three blocks. They paid $900 and sold it for $250. They purchased a truck at the dealership in 2015.

Around the same time, Luis and Bessie started volunteering for Many Meals, a program of SPIRIT of Santa Paula. They were a great team and helped for seven years. When Luis's health worsened, they had to retire. Their days are now simple and they look forward to Sundays at church in the park.

Bessie resolved to learn to read at the age of 60. She was at the library several days a week and was so proud when she could put sentences together and read a book.

Luis's son spent many years in prison and was released in 2020. Luis was so proud to see his son again and asked if we could help him find a job. His son was smart and presented well. He was energetic, tidy and thoughtful. He was given a position at Harvard Shelter. But it wasn't long before the life he lived in prison caught up with him, as did his old friends and old habits. Luis's son was dismissed from that job and has been in and out of jail since then.

We are still in touch with Luis and Bessie. They are an important part of our history, and are so much the story of people in the economic margins of our world. There's little movement for people living in grinding poverty. Luis and Bessie are among the lucky ones who were able to pool their meager funds and agree to live simply, just so they could survive together. And, the good news is they were married in July 2023.

Bessie and Luis had a unique story of homelessness, married to others and children with a variety of needs. They attracted the attention of many people in a local church and became volunteers at the local pantry, food rescue and Sunday at the park. After 10 years of companionship, they married at the First Presbyterian Church on July 15, 2023. Every bride is beautiful.

Chapter Twenty

ADDICTION AND MENTAL ILLNESS

The percentage of people addicted to drugs in the shelter is probably 80 percent. Of the people on the street, it's probably closer to 90 percent, because they can't cope otherwise. Generally, they are on the street, because they are addicts. And the minute they get their fix, they are out looking for money or something to steal, so they can get their next one.

We have explicit rules stating no drugs or drug use is allowed in the shelter. If they are high and go right to bed and right to sleep, I don't do anything about it. If they come in and they're out of control and yelling, we call 911 to get them out of here. We got burned with case manager Sabriana expertly guiding a belligerent person out the door. So now, we have to tailor our strategy with the police. The chief told us, you have to call 911. Well, we did that and no one came for 15 minutes, while this man was behaving dangerously with a four-year-old at his elbow. The young man who disarmed the gunman at the dance hall in Alhambra was invited to President Biden's State of the Union address and sat in the gallery. Surely, he saved lives. But maybe Sabriana did, too.

Addiction and mental illness are the bad boys of homelessness. Addiction can lead to homelessness for several reasons. Addiction can cause people to prioritize drug use over other basic needs, such as paying rent or bills, leading to financial instability and eventually eviction or foreclosure.

Additionally, addiction can lead to job loss as individuals struggle to maintain employment, due to absenteeism, decreased productivity or other issues. Without a steady income, they may struggle to afford housing and end up homeless. They see it happening, but don't believe it's coming.

Addiction strains relationships with family and friends, leading to a lack of support and potential housing options. People who struggle with addiction may also face discrimination and stigma, making it more difficult to secure housing and other basic needs. Their rental track record follows them.

Finally, homelessness can further exacerbate addiction, by exposing individuals to a range of new stressors and risks, such as exposure to violence, illness or exploitation, which can make it even more difficult to overcome addiction and rebuild their lives. They want help, but they don't want to do the work of sobriety.

Shelters become havens for drug users, because they have a bed, three meals, showers and laundry services. They can go off property and use, then return without evidence of being under the influence.

This is where case management becomes essential. Workers with lived experience are easily able to identify someone under the influence, and are charged with setting goals and a six-month case plan. The COVID-19 pandemic years prolonged the time guests could remain sheltered and they became very comfortable. As the economy opened and people began moving around, it was easier to establish a case plan.

By that time, however, some guests had been at Harvard for almost three years, and they felt they owned the bed. The balance of affirming and informing is very delicate. If a case manager loses relationship with a guest, the task of moving them on becomes harder. The push-pull of personal responsibility and case management is exposed for what it is—hard and harder.

Mental Health in the Shelter

Mental illness is one of many potential factors that can contribute to homelessness, but it is not the sole cause. Homelessness is typically the result of a complex interplay of multiple factors, including economic hardship, lack of affordable housing, lack of social support, substance abuse, domestic violence and systemic inequalities.

Mental illness can be a contributing factor to homelessness, as it may impair an individual's ability to work, maintain social relationships and manage finances. People with mental illness may also face discrimination and stigma that can limit their access to housing and employment opportunities. Sadly, it can be masked and it's difficult to identify, until the breakdown comes, often in acts of violence toward others or themselves.

However, it is important to note that most people with mental illness do not become homeless, and many people who are homeless do not have a diagnosed mental illness. Therefore, it is crucial to take a holistic approach, which addresses the various factors that contribute to homelessness, including mental health services, affordable housing and supportive social services, often called "wrap-around services."

The biggest challenge in addressing mental illness is the stigma and the difficulty of admitting "something is wrong with me." The other big challenge is for them to remember their appointments. Mental illness in a homeless shelter is a stigma and red flag for shelter managers charged with providing a safe environment for guests and staff. Behavioral health counselors are tasked with the responsibility of obtaining housing for their clients. When a call comes from a clinician, we must assess the client's ability to adapt to shelter life.

In reality, no one needs shelter more than someone with mental health challenges. They need sleep, rest, food, showers, clean clothes, discipline, order and structure. These are also the things they resist.

As time goes on in the shelter, despite all of our efforts to help young people with job interviews, job applications, getting their first ID cards, drivers' license and social security benefits, they lose hope. That's because we all know the reality—there is no housing to transition to. Even if there was, without some kind of a job, where a third of their income can go to rent, there's just no place to go. I watch the atmosphere in the building settle like a cold, damp blanket over everyone. You can feel the heaviness.

This is most common with the men in the shelter, because they grow to be lazy and rely on alcohol and drugs to numb down. They have too many fronts to tackle, in order to achieve the goal of permanent housing. Sobriety is hard. Addiction is hard. We often say, "Choose your hard."

Getting the paperwork together is hard, but we help with that. They get cleaned up and go to an interview, then wait for disappointment. Even if they do get a job, how do they get to work? All of that becomes a toxic mixture, adding to the elements of depression.

I was asked to speak at a housing conference this year to address housing issues. Close to 400 people attended, including developers, junior leaders, elected officials, bankers, city planners and housing advocates. In one of the early planning sessions, I mentioned the problem of depression among shelter guests. People have given up on finding a place to live and they settle back in, figuring the search is a long haul.

The planners decided to have a breakout session in the program for this topic, and they put me in charge. No one came to my session, except service providers. I concluded it was due to the fact that there is no manageable answer, and depression in a shelter is not a sexy topic. I know people lose patience with the homeless population in general. Many believe if they weren't so lazy, they wouldn't be homeless, and that they can be housed if they choose. The public has become very judgmental. I'm still pondering why not one person came to my session to hear about this problem.

The Progression of Addiction

At least a dozen homeless people have died in our area in the last 15 months. The deaths range from heart attacks to infections to overdoses and alcohol poisoning. The body knows how to heal itself, but it can't fight off death by itself. It needs rest, hydration, sanitary conditions and medical care.

The body can take a lot of abuse, but not for a long period of time. Many of our guests who deal with this enslavement end up spiraling over time. Many began using in their teens, and yes, it began with smoking pot. As they slip in their school work and separate from family relationships, they seek comfort and support with like-minded students and friends in the same age group. They soon become fully dependent on others, and the road to perdition widens.

In the spiritual realm of mental health at Harvard Shelter, I regularly refer to the ease of traveling the wide road, and the challenges of the narrow road.

Sobriety is hard work. Most of us can't imagine giving up our morning coffee, let alone the craving and the necessity for the drug hit. No one can focus on working very long after the last hit begins to subside.

The HUD model for solving homelessness is housing first. Many know housing allows them to continue their habit, while sheltered, and it is counterproductive. What we know is, without housing, there is almost no hope.

Worst Case Scenarios

Adan was one of the more charming men living on the streets. He spent as much time in jail as out. I received many calls from Adan, from Todd Road jail, looking forward to seeing me again with promises that, "This time will be different."

In my last conversation with Adan, prior to his release, I made him promise to go directly to Harvard Shelter, without detours and side trips to the river. That didn't happen and we never saw him again. He died of an overdose in the very place that tripped him up, over and over.

Such a waste of human potential. One life to live is no joke.

Despite mounting evidence to the contrary, there are many success stories of people moving on from Harvard Shelter. Some have gone to 18-month rehab programs, some to sober living homes, assisted living facilities or with family in apartments. Some have gone back to the streets to live their life without rules, other than their own. Many have died, leaving us with a sense of not having done enough.

Shelter directors are tasked with the responsibility of the well-being of the employees, who suffer when someone fails to leave Harvard for a good place. This is when I remind them, "If you did your best, that is all you can do."

And then I wonder what more I could have done. My own benchmark is to do my best. I am generally my own counselor with the words from scripture, 1 Corinthians 10:31, "So whether you eat or drink or whatever you do, do it all for the glory of God."

Chapter Twenty-One

LIFE AND DEATH IN THE SHELTER

Navigating the ebb and flow of life and death within the walls of a homeless shelter is an unparalleled experience that intertwines compassion with stark reality. Within this microcosm of society, residents and staff alike grapple with the constant reminders of mortality amidst the struggle for survival. The shelter becomes a haven, where stories of resilience and vulnerability intersect, as individuals facing the harshness of homelessness seek solace and sustenance.

From celebrating small victories, to mourning untimely losses, the shelter's atmosphere oscillates between camaraderie and somber reflection, highlighting the profound significance of compassion in the face of life's most challenging circumstances.

Following are two examples of our constant reminders.

Dr. Novak Vukotic was staying in a skilled nursing facility in the neighboring community of Fillmore, while recovering from cancer treatments. When he was strong enough to leave, the discharge manager asked if we would take him into Harvard Shelter. Their driver delivered him one afternoon, and we were all surprised. Novak was a tall, aging gentleman in his early 80s who was a retired physician from Montenegro, in old Yugoslavia.

He looked around the room and assumed it was his last stop, so he settled in and became a good citizen of Harvard Shelter. We arranged for a hospital bed for several reasons, primarily because we wanted him to be as comfortable as possible.

We learned he had been a janitor at St. Sebastian Church and lived in a modest one-bedroom apartment near the church. When Novak entered the hospital, he stayed for a year. He had a housing voucher, and the rent on his apartment was being paid. But, due to his absence, the landlord moved everything out of the apartment and rented it to someone else. She had visited him in the facility and knew his plans to return home, but she acted anyway.

His shock and dismay about his new circumstances were almost overwhelming. But he did his best to make friends and tolerate the kids, even when trying to sleep during the day. He still needed regular visits to the oncologist for treatment. I wanted to be attentive to him, so I took him to each appointment and of course the nurse greeted us with, "And, how are you today?"

After 10 months of treatment, he knew his days were short. His doctor was aware of Novak's living situation, and he made arrangements for Novak to return to a skilled nursing facility, instead of to us.

Novak died in February 2022. His phone and personal papers were put in his body bag, and he was housed in the hospital morgue, until arrangements could be made with his family in Montenegro. There was nothing they could do, so Novak was cremated and buried in a charity grave, in a cemetery in Ventura.

Novak was a loner. Due to his size and distinguished manner, most people left him alone. He ate by himself and kept to himself. His English was impressive, but his accent made it difficult to understand every word. He had an unusual ability to remain cheerful, despite his circumstances.

He never married and always hoped he could find someone to share his life with when he came to the U.S. There was a woman at one time, but not enough in the relationship to warrant marriage.

Such irony. He was a man with the highest level of training as a physician who fled his home country to find a better life. He expressed contempt for the Germans and because he had to leave his country. The breakup of Yugoslavia was complicated. Novak was polite, but lonely, and he, like most people, referred to his health condition as his "damn cancer," because it changed everything.

Fortunately, he had medical insurance and a small pension. He used an old flip phone and never learned to text. He often asked for extra meat, because he needed protein to accelerate his healing.

He was always tidy, kept his bed made and clothes folded. He slept most of the day, and when it was time to leave Harvard Shelter, he had trouble being steady on his feet. He left us as quietly as he came.

There are many things about managing a shelter that bring satisfaction and elements of joy. Serving Novak in his last days is one of them.

His sister was contacted by the medical examiner in Montenegro and they provided my contact information to her. She called and begged for any scrap of information that would help her live peacefully with Novak's demise. We spoke twice and I assured her he had been in good hands until the end. She wept and thanked me.

Juan was a likable young man and didn't cause any problems. He was 21 years old and came to us as a result of an extreme domestic violence charge by a family member. He threatened to kill his mother and she had a restraining order against him. Prior to any intake, we do as much research as we can about everyone's background. That's when we discovered the incident through an online search. Juan spent some time in prison. His parole officer tried to assure us it was an isolated incident and Juan would be safe to have at Harvard Shelter. Obviously, he was not allowed to live with his family and, as far as we knew, there was no relationship.

Juan was a meth user. It complicates everyone's life, including those who care for him.

Addiction to methamphetamines, commonly known as meth, can have a profound and devastating impact on individuals and their loved ones. Meth is a powerful stimulant drug that affects the central nervous system, leading to intense euphoria and increased energy levels. However, the regular use of meth can quickly lead to addiction, due to its highly addictive nature and the chemical changes it induces in the brain.

Here are some characteristics and effects commonly associated with meth addiction:

Cravings and Compulsive Use: Meth addiction often involves intense cravings for the drug. Users may feel an overwhelming desire to use meth, leading to compulsive drug-seeking behavior. This can result in a loss of control over drug use, as individuals prioritize obtaining and using meth over other aspects of their life. An addict needs a fix or a high every two hours. As soon as they get a fix, they start thinking about the second one.

With continued use, the body develops a physical dependence to meth. This means the individual's body adapts to the presence of the drug and requires it to function normally. Withdrawal symptoms, such as fatigue, depression, anxiety, irritability and intense drug cravings can occur when meth use is stopped. One street person told me the effects of failure to get that fix is something he wouldn't wish on his worst enemy. I had to ponder that.

Over time, meth users may develop tolerance to the drug, requiring larger doses to achieve the desired effects. Escalating use can lead to a dangerous cycle of increased drug consumption, which can have severe health consequences.

Methamphetamine abuse can lead to numerous physical and mental health problems. These may include cardiovascular issues, dental problems (known as "meth mouth"), skin infections, malnutrition, weight loss, insomnia, paranoia, hallucinations, anxiety, depression and cognitive impairment.

Meth addiction can lead to strained relationships, isolation, financial difficulties, legal issues and problems at work or school. The intense focus on obtaining and using the drug can cause individuals to neglect responsibilities and engage in risky behaviors. They are a challenge in shelters, because they have no filter when it's time to use again.

Meth addiction often takes a toll on a person's emotional well-being. Users may experience mood swings, irritability, aggression and a sense of emptiness or depression when not using the drug. While Juan knew he had to be on good behavior, he often failed to demonstrate it, because the cravings overtook every thought.

It's important to note that meth addiction is a treatable condition, and recovery is possible with appropriate professional help and support. However, it's difficult, because the withdrawal effects and the necessary rewiring of the brain create dramatic mood swings, as the body learns to cope without the drug it has depended upon.

One night during the COVID-19 pandemic, a known drug dealer rode his bicycle onto the property and Juan ran out to meet him. There was clearly an exchange of something. Juan left the property, but came back in time to go to bed.

Sometime during that quiet night, Juan died in his bed. He was discovered at 6 a.m. by one of the moms, who noticed something wrong. There was a call to 911 with a full police and fire department response. Juan was dead.

We believe those sleeping next to Juan may have heard him gurgling in the night, but ignored it. The supervisor that night noticed nothing out of the ordinary.

A review of the cameras showed the visit. We contacted police to tell them about the video, but they did not come to Harvard to see it. There are some officers who are numb to the personal plight of homeless people. Others are most interested in causing no harm.

Juan's death came and went. The next day, his parents demanded to meet with me. They accused us of poisoning their son. That was a first-time experience. My training as a fire chaplain helped me respond appropriately. His sister did not want financial help from us and made it clear they wanted no relationship either. The family held a service, but we were not included, which was another first. When a death occurs among our network, we are always included.

Some weeks later, we were notified that the cause of death was fentanyl. Overdose. Again.

Chapter Twenty-Two

BAD NEWS ON A GOOD DAY—THE DAILY SALVOS

There's enough sorrow in the world to make all of us cry every day. Every day, our phone rings with pleas from distraught people asking for help with utility bills, rent, car repairs, medicine or gas cards. The calls come from mothers with children living in cars, mothers spending their last night in a motel, and even a teacher helping a family with four kids living in a house with no heat. Police officers and sheriff's deputies also call us about people on the streets.

Repeated exposure to the suffering, violence and abuse homeless people face can lead to feelings of stress, burnout and compassion fatigue. Additionally, the lack of funding and resources for homeless shelters adds to frustration and hopelessness among the people who serve and work in the shelter environment. Despite these challenges, many shelter workers—my own staff included—continue to provide crucial support to homeless individuals and families. Recognizing and addressing the impact of trauma on the people who work in this field is important.

In 2022, a valuable case manager had to step back from her work, overwhelmed by stress and burnout. Jessica Lucas did amazing work for so many. Her number was on speed dial for agencies, referral networks and shelter guests. When she left, I knew it would be hard to find someone with her passion and commitment to the well-being of others.

This work is hard and the setbacks are beyond disappointing. Jessica is now dedicating herself to finishing her master's degree in social work, and she has many opportunities ahead. I cannot commend her enough or begin to tell you all the hundreds of ways she improved people's lives.

***

Here are just a few examples of the calls we get on a daily basis. Knowing and seeing these things takes a toll on caregivers. Pray for us.

> *"My car was towed and everything I own is in it. Will you help me?" Is it registered? "No." Is it insured? "No." Do you know the value of the car? "About $1,500."*

> *"My daughter and I have only eaten Top Ramen for two days. Can you help us?"*

> *"My wife left me two months ago. She has a boyfriend, and I can't pay the rent by myself. I have a two-year-old son. Can you help me?"*

> *"I can't pay the rent. My landlord is being nice, but wants her money. I have three children and I'm a single parent. My mom takes care of the kids so I can work. Can you help me?"*

"I fell off my bicycle and broke my arm. I am homeless and on probation. Can I stay at your shelter?"

"I am desperate. I had my wallet stolen and my rent money was in it. Can you help me? Also, our dog is sick and I don't know how to help her."

"I was living with my mom, but she is in a senior's neighborhood, and I have to leave. I have two kids who need to get to school. I'm scared and desperate. Can you help me?"

A call from Margaret: *"If you can help, please call me back. My brother is an amputee and just became homeless. He has nowhere to go. He has a small dog he is attached to and cannot part with him. Can you help?"*

A call from Barbara: *"I am 61 years old and disabled. I have an inoperable brain tumor and three auto-immune diseases. I am dizzy from the medication and weak on one side. I live with my ex-daughter-in-law and she and her new boyfriend are kicking me out on Sept. 30. Can someone help me?"*

A call from Jennifer: *"Would it be a good idea for me to come to your shelter? I live with my parents, but we are always in crisis."*

A call from Lynn: *"My son is homeless and he's 26 years old. I'm desperate and so is he. Can you help him?"*

A call from Dad: *"My son just went AWOL from the Jackson House. He's dehydrated now and I don't know where he is. If he tries to check into your shelter, please call me."*

"I am a single mom with two kids, and we are living in my car. Can you help me? I am from Ventura."

"Hi Kay, I got your info from a friend of mine from homeless services. I need financial assistance. I left my husband, because of domestic violence and when he left, he took my envelope of money that I had stashed for rent and bills. I won't be able to afford my rent, all my utilities are past due and I have no food. I really need help. If you can help or if you can refer me to places that can, I would really appreciate it. I actually got my current rental from your real estate agency. Dina was my contact. Please let me know if you're able to help me."

"Hi Kay, this is Mara. I heard you help people. I only have two days left in my apartment and I will be homeless. I am 62 years old and I have a parrot who is 47 years old. Can I stay at your shelter? I am from Oxnard."

"Good evening, Kay Wilson. My name is Deborah Salazar. I attend your food share on Saturdays and Many Meals on Wednesdays. I live in a duplex apartment and someone deliberately set the apartment next door to me on fire. My apartment was saved, but most of my clothes were in my backyard waiting to be washed. When firefighters turned the fire off, they ruined most of my clothes. Meaning everything. Under clothes, pajamas, socks, sweats and jackets. Basically everything. I seen someone was gonna donate plus size clothes. If it's possible for me to get some, I'd truly appreciate it. Here is my phone number: 805-000-0000. Feel free to get at me please. I don't have transportation and I am very sick with an inflamed hernia, which I'll be having surgery on in the next two weeks. Thank you. God bless you. Much love and appreciation. Deborah."

"I'm calling from the psych ward at Glendale Hospital. Do you have a bed for me?"

"My name is Denise and I am 82 years old. Your friend, Merl, told me to call you. I am in a motel and only a day left in the motel. I can stay in a friend's mobile home, but

143

she is a hoarder and there is no room for me. I get $800 a month. Can you help me?"

✷✷✷

A woman called and asked if her 80-year-old uncle could stay at the shelter for a while. I asked her to explain. She said he came from up north to be with his family, hoping he could stay with one of his brothers or sisters. But, she said, *"We don't have room for him."* I pressed her for more information, because this is not usually the dialogue I have with someone who needs a bed in a homeless shelter. I told her I would have to think about it, because the shelter is for Santa Paula people only.

However, I was thinking about an 80-year-old man, somewhere on the streets of Oxnard or Ventura, the cities where his family lives. The next day, the family dropped him off at the shelter when I wasn't there. When I arrived, I was astonished. He came without permission. After obtaining his niece's phone number, I called her, but was put on the phone with his brother. I was not as nice as I usually am, asking many questions about why and how they could do this. I learned he has a sister who lives alone, but her children don't want him there. So, he is at the shelter, listening to his music and programs on his phone with earbuds in place. How can this be?

This is just a sampling of the daily onslaught of requests that come into the SPIRIT of Santa Paula. The weight of listening to harrowing stories of desperation, substance abuse, mental health struggles and life threatening circumstances is a blow against the heart. Service providers, who are committed to helping, often find themselves grappling with limited resources and the heartbreaking reality that they can't always provide the comprehensive support required. Balancing empathy with the frustration of systemic limitations becomes a delicate tightrope.

144

This collective burden underscores the critical need for accessible mental health support, for both those who seek assistance and those who provide it in these challenging environments.

After Jessica left, Sabriana Marrufo assumed the role of case manager. We can't be without one. Sabriana has the essential classification of "lived experience" and she knows how to navigate the various systems that lead people to wellness and housing. At the time of this writing, she has been with SPIRIT for approximately three years, and her family was in the shadows of homelessness for many months.

She had been serving as SPIRIT's shelter manager, and learned the ropes by helping people navigate out of Harvard and meeting weekly with Jessica. The federal model is "Housing First," so people are sheltered while they receive services, treatment and, hopefully, an escort to rehab.

Nomi Marrufo is now the general manager of SPIRIT of Santa Paula, and she is responsible for all operations, facilities maintenance, guest safety and welfare, food rescue, food sourcing and food pantries. What goes with this are tasks like new batteries in the clocks, keeping supplies ordered, replacing broken legs on chairs and locating the last person who had the storeroom key.

Nomi has also been with SPIRIT since the early days in several capacities. There is no substitute for lived experience and common sense. Nomi sees the big picture and manages to fit the puzzle pieces together at the right time.

It's amazing to find such excellence within our small group of dedicated employees. The future of SPIRIT is in good hands.

Chapter Twenty-Three

WHEN DOES HOMELESSNESS BEGIN?

It's tempting to continue to cuss and discuss the mess that represents homelessness in America. I suggest we also focus on prevention, and ask, "How did this happen?"

No one is born with a plan to become homeless. No one is born without a dream of living the good life, whatever they perceive it to be.

I believe homelessness begins with the first stumble, followed by other stumbles. I have yet to meet anyone who didn't have a first birthday, accompanied by some kind of celebration. They had their first Christmas and a first glimpse of Santa Claus. They had a first day of school, typically filled with excitement and fear.

There must be a series of small steps leading someone into the realm of homelessness, which is compounded by addiction.

Let's talk about a boy named Chance. Was there a day when he made one single decision that would lead to an unraveled life? Did it begin with a refusal to get out of bed in time for school? Or, maybe a refusal to brush his teeth that led to complications later on? When did he first refuse to complete a homework assignment, participate in sports or join a club? How much time was spent staring at screens?

Chance quit school when he was 16, and all he could think about was buying a car. He began hanging with kids who had similar ambitions and lack of vision. He got his first DUI that set him up for future setbacks—fines, penalties, canceled insurance, expired registration and eventually the car was towed.

When did he start asking friends and family to "borrow" money, never with the intention of repayment? Since he didn't graduate from high school, his job options were limited, and now he has no transportation.

Did Chance neglect his teeth until the pain overwhelmed him and he found relief in a can of beer, which became a six-pack, and then a case? Did he opt for a marijuana hit, which, whether you agree or not, led to meth or heroin or cocaine, all with the intention of medicating and covering the real pain?

Chance did not register to vote, finish high school or look for ways to improve his situation. It became easy to slide in with like-minded friends, attempt a burglary and party the night away.

Chance started stealing money from his family when they were away, and then the family treasures, which would be sold for pennies.

This accumulation of stumbles leads to a collapse. Chance was lucky to rent an apartment with some friends, but it wasn't long before they couldn't pay the rent. The landlord was tired of the mess and began the eviction process.

An eviction begins a trail of disasters. No one wants to take a chance on Chance, because he's proven himself unreliable. His credit report is trashed and so is his reputation within the realm of references.

Another example is David. He was a stellar football player at Santa Paula High School, a good student, popular and owned one of the fanciest cars in the senior class. One day, someone introduced him to a substance that triggered the tragic spiral into homelessness.

David now wanders the streets of Santa Paula, pulling someone's trash can filled with things he has stolen. Recently, the owner of the Santa Paula Inn called and said she wanted to know who David was, because he frequented their business near the commercial district. It's a common occurrence for people in the community to call me with complaints about the behaviors of homeless people.

I always try to portray the best side of any homeless person, if I know their history, without ever excusing their bad behavior. I find it softens a person's irritation if they can connect with their humanity.

In David's case, I shared his history, and she was surprised to learn about David's life before drugs. She viewed him with new eyes, but I warned her not to trust him to do the right thing.

Not long after that conversation, a man called, who was told I might be able to help him with a theft. A man of David's description was seen getting into his car and taking his laptop and other electronics. That man was a lawyer called to town for business.

I told him to call the police and report that David had stolen from him, and they would know where to find him. I gave him two locations. Sure enough, David was seen at the gazebo near the Chamber of Commerce. He was smart enough to stash the laptop in the trash can, which surprisingly enough, was retrieved by its owner.

Is there hope for David? The answer is yes and no. There's no hope if he doesn't change, and there is hope if he does. I believe each of us gets to choose how we live our lives. I can't do for them what only they can do for themselves, but the SPIRIT of Santa Paula staff is there to help when they are ready.

I cannot long for sobriety harder than they do. Is it hard to be an addict on the streets? Yes, it is. Is it hard to get sober and stay that way? It absolutely is.

When they argue with me about how hard that part is, I challenge them to "choose their hard." It's common for some to stay intoxicated and high, because it's too hard to go to rehab and detox to re-calibrate their brains. But not going to rehab is hard, too.

Ten years on the street with an addiction is a long time, but only a segment of a lifetime free of addiction's chains.

David is one of many children. His brother was staying at Harvard Shelter and stole the company credit card. He put new tires on his car, gas in the tank and took himself to lunch at McDonald's. I've learned to be a detective. We were able to trace the charges and who signed, along with obtaining a description of the driver and the car. Sometimes, they are smarter than we are, but not for long. At least he wasn't at the Ritz. We caught him and got the card back. The police figured the DA wouldn't do much about it, so he got away with that one.

Many of the other children in David's family have resided at Harvard. One year, we had grandma, four of her adult children and eight of her grandchildren.

One Christmas, one of the mothers spent a lot of money buying all the family members matching pajamas. I'm sure it was with the hope of making everyone feel normal, despite their living situation.

They were in the shelter for a long time. Their little girl was the first to get COVID-19 in December 2019, before we knew what it was.

David's brother, while a guest at Harvard, got a job washing windows of office buildings in Westlake. He said he worked at night. He had been on good behavior and was helping around the shelter. He asked me to loan him money, so he could get a car and get to work on time, not relying on others. I thought about it for a long time and finally agreed. It was $1,500. He never registered the car, and it was finally towed. There went the job, the car and the money. He was later arrested for receiving stolen goods.

It's hard to not believe in people. I've learned many things in this work, and one of them is to give money without the expectation of being repaid. In fairness, there have been some good decisions. It's hard to tell if it's a good one, until it isn't. Perhaps that's what people think when they make decisions, which unfortunately leads them into a downward spiral. The best we can do is guide them to make better decisions in the future.

Chapter Twenty-Four

SOMEONE ELSE'S PROBLEM

It was a Saturday evening, when a man named Matthew called from a Long Beach number, seeking shelter for a friend in Santa Paula. As he described his friend, I asked if he was talking about Linda Rictor. I told him I knew her, and I had been talking to her all week. She was trying to rent a home from my property management company. He said his call was on her behalf.

I've known Linda for many years. She was living with her 80-year-old sister, but was asked to leave. Several years ago, I received a police call to assist with a domestic violence matter between the two sisters. That's when I met Linda and Jody.

Jody called on Wednesday and begged me to take her sister into the shelter. I asked Jody how she could kick her sister out, knowing Linda was on the street, living in her car. Jody said, "She's too much trouble and too hard to have around." I find it so odd that people assume a shelter is a suitable place for those they can't tolerate.

Linda worked for Von's for many years and can go back to work if she wants. Linda is a challenge. She can be very combative when under the influence. While we are a low barrier shelter, thought must be given to the safety and well-being of others already there. I hesitated to take Linda in, because of past combative (sometimes violent) behavior.

Our shelter is at capacity, except for one male who did not return as expected. Due to interior construction in process, at the time of writing this, beds have been moved in crazy places. I cannot begin making bed moves at this hour. No one owns a bed at Harvard, but nesting provides a sense of safety and peace.

During the lengthy discussion with the caller from Long Beach, he expressed frustration at my reluctance to take Linda in, asking why our shelter exists. I told him all Ventura County shelters are full and have rules about intake times. I gave the county information on 211, but he pressed me on why we exist. No explanation of safety or capacity was going to satisfy him.

Some days, words cut deeply. So, I turned the tables and asked him how many bedrooms he has. He sputtered a bit, then said he lives in a nice, two-bedroom condo, and he and his wife both work. He mentioned "nice" to indicate his neighborhood was not suitable for the likes of Linda. He further justified not taking her in, by stating it would not be fair to take her away from her social center in Santa Paula—as though she had one. Linda has no particular social environment in Santa Paula, and I'm sure she would welcome her own bedroom in any town—even in Long Beach.

Our conversation was getting uncomfortable, and I told him I would consider taking her in. When I called Linda, she said she was scared and living in her car. Shelter staff let me know there were only two top bunks available. Nomi agreed to set up a cot, and we would work on the shuffle the next morning.

Linda was having difficulty finding our location, probably due to the wine. She called me twice to ask for directions. She had to park on the street and walk in. There are few lights near our location. I reminded her to limit the items she brings in. They want to bring everything they own, so they feel nested and secure with their own things around them.

It's a constant battle to stop them from buying stuff at the thrift store and loading up their assigned bins with their personal items.

The caller from Long Beach reminded me how God provided for Mary and Joseph to have a place to stay. I am well aware of this story and it is largely why we do this in the first place.

Equally fascinating is the common comment that very few people ever take someone into their own home. Everyone wants someone to do something, but few people will take on an inconvenience. Yes, we are a shelter, but without rules and protocols, you invite chaos.

I recently read a statement by an unknown author: "Don't tell anyone Jesus loves them, until you are willing to love them."

People are homeless for many reasons. Most often, it has to do with challenging relationships, bad decisions and equally bad behavior. Substance abuse is the result of many bad decisions leading to homelessness. Mental illness can be the result of substance abuse and of the effects of homelessness. Few of us can imagine how out of control our lives would be without a place of our own to eat, shower and sleep.

People with a home, an income and access to privacy have the same substance abuse problems that people in shelters have. I have friends who are alcoholics, but nobody really suffers from it, because they do it in their home. Driving is an issue, of course. However, because they have access to privacy, it's okay for them. In my group setting, where there is no privacy, they are judged and harmed by the stigma of something that exists in secret, in the rest of the population.

The city of Los Angeles has approximately 65,000 people living on city streets. What will we do when that number is 75,000? More importantly, what will we do with the people who say they would rather live on the street than in any kind of housing? They have that right, and until they are declared "gravely disabled," they will continue to live on the streets. That's another topic.

Newly elected Mayor Karen Bass is committed to solving this problem, and she's finding it a slow go, partly due to the bureaucracy. And partly due to something we never expected—many don't actually want to be housed.

Those are the people who love the drug more than a bed. They cannot follow rules and are obsessed with the next fix.

Linda struggles with alcohol still, but is back to work. She left Harvard in August 2023, because she was able to rent a room. She wants to be reunited with her cat, but the local animal rescue foundation is concerned, because the cat is recovering from a long period of neglect.

We had to take her keys away from her for a time, because we knew she was driving under the influence. She was cooperative and timed her drinking, so when it was time to test her, she would almost always pass.

Like all of us, Linda has a choice to make. It comes down to how well she wants to live her life. Her time with us stabilized her, and she made some lasting friendships. We see her at Von's and I am so grateful we took her in. She is now living the life she dreamed of. It's up to her.

Chapter Twenty-Five

Many Don't Want to Be Housed

Los Angeles has a very aggressive plan to house every homeless person. There are a lot of empty buildings in L.A., and they are trying to refurbish them for housing. However, many of these people refuse the offer of housing. They say they are fine where they are. They will take money for food and cigarettes, but they don't want to leave where they're comfortable, in order to be housed.

So, what does America do with and for this part of our population? What is our responsibility to integrate them into what we know as normal to help them lead functioning and productive lives? Humans are designed to work and take care of families, unless we/they are mentally challenged. Bringing the terrible, frustrating scenario into my own shelter, I have young men who don't want to get a driver's license. They don't want to finish their high school diploma. They don't want a job. They are happy to lie on a bed, looking at their phone all day long and actually do nothing.

Ryan is one example. He is a sweet man, probably 28 years old, is overweight, an alcoholic and suffers from extreme anxiety. It's so bad, he has to go outside, where he shakes uncontrollably. One day, he told the shelter manager, "I need you to go get my medicine at CVS." She said, "Why? Do you need it right now?" He said, "I should have gotten it yesterday."

This personality type doesn't do what they're supposed to do, then they make demands on others to get it done. They blame anyone else, excuse themselves for any responsibility and place demands on our staff.

We finally got him to agree to go into Jackson House, a local 10-day treatment center for mental health issues, which drinking exacerbates. He was supposed to get a rapid COVID-19 test the day before his entrance. He didn't get it, because he had other plans. He has a crush on a girl in the shelter, and she decided to take her kids out of school, so they could play miniature golf all day long. His decision prevented him from entering Jackson House.

What do we do about that behavior? And, he's just one. Imagine the challenge of thousands of people like that? What is society going to do? Can we let this worsen by doing nothing?

Los Angeles has 65,000 people on the streets as of this writing. My solution would be to identify the most productive 10 percent and launch them into a new, model environment. The goal would be to manage everyone, getting them ready for living independently.

The rest may languish for a while, but may be motivated by the success of others. They may want to be part of the next 10 percent. I'm glad I'm not the mayor of Los Angeles. In our community of Santa Paula, people are living in the West End River area, where they can look up and see the houses on the hill. The homeless refer to "those people up there" in the same way we refer to them as "those people down there." They say, "I don't want to have to go up there and be with those people." I don't know if it's because they might have to work, or explain themselves or have meetings with someone. They have a solution for everything, such as a 5-gallon paint bucket buried in the ground to use as a toilet. When it's full, they throw dirt on top of it and go dig another hole for another bucket. That's what they're doing to our riverbeds.

The human services side of this issue is almost impossible. I don't know what percentage of the homeless population is content with the way they are. I do know they have lost all relationships with family. And, I don't know what our cities are going to look like if we don't get them off the streets, where they are peeing and pooping on the sidewalks. That alone is a major health hazard for everyone.

Mayor Karen Bass is a very smart woman with vision and good ideas about how to get people off the street. She has been given $50 million dollars in non-discretionary funds to do it. She is now facing the problem of people who don't want to be housed. Of course, when you're super medicated, you don't care where you are. That's a problem we never thought we would have. We always thought the problem was where we would house them. Due to this discovery, many are criticizing her plans.

What do we do with people who are happy to live on the streets? You can't shoot them. You can't starve them. We are not that kind of country. However, serious neglect occurs in other parts of the world. I've seen pictures in Calcutta of dead bodies on the street and no one does anything about it.

News reports state rents in California have stopped rising, but they're still insane. For $2,000 a month, you get a studio apartment or maybe a small one bedroom. Most families don't have $2,000 a month to spend on rent. Karen Bass has to address that problem, too. So do the landlords in Ventura County.

Consequences of Inaction

There are serious consequences to doing nothing about this issue. Kids are not getting to school, so we are creating a new generation of lost people. COVID-19 initiated that. When kids are not in school learning what they need to know, how can they become productive adults—and parents? What will their needs be? Will they be satisfied with what the government gives them? And how long can the government sustain that drain? Will that mean retirement is delayed, because we all have to work longer to pay the taxes that need to be generated? Do we take care of this population group, who are not taking care of themselves, in a way our quality of life is minimized?

Homelessness is affecting every socio-economic category in our society. We all have to work harder and longer. Will the elite generation run the government? There will always be the elites. There are many smart kids in our schools and many dedicated parents raising their kids to be productive. However, we are creating a new economic class that needs to be governed. They won't have anything to pass along to the next generation.

I often wonder, what do the snowy northern states do for their homeless people during the winter? The weather has been insane around our country. It's a real hardship, even in Santa Paula's temperate climate, because it's been so cold this year at night. But people are not freezing to death on our streets. If somebody is on the streets in Michigan, they likely do.

I recently took three little girls from the shelter to see *Lion King* in Hollywood, and afterwards, we went to McDonald's. There were homeless tents all around the area and the smell was really third world. I noticed people walking around tents, ignoring them and driving by. No one was honking. We've all become numb to these sites.

While we were ordering, a young woman came in and stood near us. I had a sense she was waiting for me to buy her dinner. I asked, "Have you eaten today?" She said, "No." So I told her to order something. As we were finishing up our order, she asked, "Can I get an apple pie?" It made me think, she's probably done this before. It may even be how she eats every day.

She could see the three little girls with me, and she asked, "What's your name?" I told her. She asked, "Why are you here?" I told her and she studied me. When I think about her, I wonder what hope there is. People are so accustomed to surviving in a low place that it becomes their new normal, and anywhere else would be abnormal.

The movie *The Soloist* is a classic example. It gives you a deeper understanding of the situation. The story revolves around Steve Lopez, an L.A. Times columnist, who found a mentally challenged homeless man, who played the cello. He followed him and got to know him over time. After building some trust, he got the man a motel room and paid for it. But the man couldn't stay there. He panicked and went back where he was comfortable, playing his cello under the freeway.

A growing percentage of the homeless are refusing housing. They will take money for food, cigarettes and other things, but they don't want to trade it for housing. What is our responsibility to force them to integrate into what we know is normal, in order to make them functioning people?

When I looked at the girl I bought dinner for at McDonald's in Hollywood, I wondered. Who is she? Where is her family? How did she get to this place? She was African American with a very dull look on her face. She had what looked like recent detailed braiding and extensions, which take skill and cost money.

I don't know what our cities are going to look like if we don't get these people off the street. They pee and poop right on the sidewalks. As I mentioned earlier, Los Angeles Mayor Karen Bass is a smart and accomplished woman. She has some good ideas for getting people off the streets, and the city has given her $50 million dollars to use at her sole discretion to solve the problem. She doesn't have to report to the city council or ask for permission. She can do whatever she thinks will work. We have reached a point when we see someone who is willing to tackle the problem, we give them a huge pot of money and say, go do it. Let us know how it turns out.

What are the consequences of doing nothing in a free society? What are the taxpayers' responsibility to the homeless? With so many people to take care of, does it mean people will have to retire later, because they have to work longer to generate the taxes needed to care for people who are not taking care of themselves? Everyone's quality of life is impacted. It affects every socio-economic category in our society. Are we creating a new class of people who are going to govern the lower classes, who don't care if they have anything, except what they need to eat? We have lots of those people in our cities.

While some people don't want to be housed, others don't want to leave the shelter. That means, I don't have a rotation of people coming in and going out. With no one leaving, the newly homeless don't have anywhere to go, because others are taking up the beds. What do we do with people who don't want to leave?

Their choice to not cooperate with case management and complete the smallest of assignments invites a bleak future. Without an income, there's no place for them to go. The affordability crisis is real. Not only are they soaking up services, they occupy a bed indefinitely. We are working on six-month plans for everyone. We remind them regularly of the potential of exit, if they have not accomplished reasonable benchmarks.

Harvard staff members and I are developing a system of benchmarks to meet if they want to stay in our shelter. We will give them six months, and if they can't check off the boxes, they will have to leave. I hope this will motivate them. If we have to escort them out the door, it brings us back to the person who would rather be homeless and on the street, rather than do anything to save themselves.

Access and Responsibility

One of the questions I asked myself long ago is, "Are we our brother's keeper?" I believe we are. I recently learned a great lesson about boundaries from author Lisa Tykherst. She speaks on setting boundaries for yourself, from a Christian perspective. Setting boundaries is difficult, because Jesus laid down his life and told others that a, "greater love has no one than this, than to lay down one's life for his friends." That means, you totally give yourself to a situation, which I have done.

But Lisa points out one of the first things God did to Adam and Eve in the Garden of Eden was to draw a big circle around the Tree of Life and say, you can have anything you want, just not fruit from this tree. That was the first boundary and it was established for their good. It was not a punishment; it was meant to keep them safe. Lisa also addresses the people around us who affect our well-being. If you are functioning at a high level and the person you're trying to help is functioning at a low level, there is danger in giving them a high level of access to you. They are not taking on the responsibility they should to have that level of access. You need to reduce their level of access to you, down to their level. That way, you create a safe boundary for yourself.

Shelter guests have high access to us, because they need it and want it. We are learning how to set boundaries for what we can give, without compromising our well-being.

I regularly talk to my staff about how we protect our hearts in this hard, hard work. When Ryan insisted he needed his medication and we needed to go get it right then, my staff asked, "When did you need it?" He said, "Yesterday." They should have said, "You should have taken the bus yesterday." He has an income of about $900 a month from the government. He can afford bus fare.

The balance of access and responsibility is an interesting way to deal with your own emotions, as well as what you allow other people to take from you. I tend to give a high level of access willingly. But there are times when I'm astonished and irritated with the demands.

My next experiment is to reduce access people have to me, according to the level of responsibility they are willing to accept. Boundaries are important to prevent being exhausted all the time, as well as feeling used and abused by those we serve.

One of my staff members has already collapsed under the weight of this kind of giving. She was driven to help people. She would be the first one to say, "Come on, Ryan, get in the car. I'll take you to get your medicine." She has said to many, "I will take you to treatment, and I will help you check in." She gave so much access to herself, without the equivalent amount of responsibility from her clients. She completely exhausted herself and had to quit. She believed she was a failure as a case worker. There is a difference between, "If I take you to treatment, will you go?" and having the client say, "If you take me to treatment, I'll go." There needs to be an even exchange of access and responsibility.

Our case manager had many successes, because she was relentless. Case management takes it, but losing her was a loss for us and for her clients.

There is a reality about the various elements of rescue, and I have experienced the negative and troublesome consequences of helping on numerous occasions. Due to my many daily contacts with people with great needs, I have learned to keep my own personal space uncomplicated. I, too, need to recover from the day, so I can love the world again tomorrow.

Chapter Twenty-Six

THE POWER OF ANGER

We know well the power of water, wind and fire. We have seen wind turn turbines, water generate electricity and fire keep us warm around the campfire. At Harvard Shelter, we see nothing good come from the power of hate. If properly focused, hate can become anger and generate action to solve a problem, preventing danger or failure.

Inside each one of us is some childhood memory of disappointment or discouragement, ranging on the spectrum of trauma. These Adverse Childhood Experiences are called ACEs. The more ACEs a child experiences, the more challenged they are to find a good footing in their adult years. Also, the case managers are challenged in finding a good path to actually help someone overcome these early adverse experiences.

Julia is a bright woman, who had an extremely challenging childhood. Both parents are now homeless and meth addicts, and her two siblings are almost equally challenged in all aspects of life.

Julia has solid brain power and wants to work. However, she can't stay current with all the elements of life that keep disaster at bay.

She's had good and responsible jobs, but can't get the car registered. She gets regular paychecks, but can't find time to get her driver's license. She has an athletic son, who is staying with a family friend, while she toughs it out at Harvard Shelter.

She bears a striking resemblance to her mother, who lives on the street, so much so, it's hard to not comment on it.

Julia is offended by any reference to her parents and resorts to the most foul language to let people know to stay out of her face, her space and shut the f-up. Her Facebook posts are enough to make you cry—or blush—as she rants in her frustration and hopelessness.

Her case manager has been working with her for two months to get a document notarized to get birth certificates. She misses notary appointments and forgets that with the passing of each day, the problem gets a little bigger and further away from resolution.

Every action plan that includes doing this or that, meets with temporary agreement, but rarely with accomplishment. The challenge we face for space at Harvard shelter with only 49 beds is to continue keeping people housed who will not, or cannot, accomplish simple tasks. The tasks lead to permanent supportive housing.

She has a housing voucher and is looking for a rental. Many believe their relationship with me is a quick and easy approval for a rental. Not so. I have landlords, who expect a proper screening and good judgment for placing them into their units.

Julia has a job, but her car was towed because she's two months behind in payments. She is frantic, mad and blaming everyone. She owed $540 and has $400. We loaned her $150, but because she doesn't have a driver's license, it takes a third party to retrieve the vehicle. Someone with a license has to go with her and receive the car.

The towing company will have a significant charge for impounding and towing the vehicle, which will be on top of what she owes to the lender.

All important papers, as well as most of her clothes and personal belongings, are still in the car. Without the ability to retrieve the vehicle, she's facing an enormous setback that won't be overcome anytime soon, creating another mountain of frustration and delay in reaching any goal.

Her way of coping with these disasters is to blast anyone in hearing distance with a cellphone in hand to those who have Messenger, Facebook and Instagram. Her most recent post states she hates the shelter. It's hard to restrain a response, but a deep breath leads to encouraging and sympathetic words. Admonishing her for using such outrageous and offensive language is not helpful. Her every expression exhibits a hopeless and helpless attitude.

Julia blames everyone else for the problems. Most of us can do this in ordinary things and may be justified, but her current circumstances are the result of failing, time after time, to take care of simple things. I remind shelter guests the best way to avoid a toothache is to brush their teeth three times a day.

So goes the remedy for catastrophe avoidance, by taking care of business as it comes. This goes for simple things like keeping documents safe, to returning phone calls, to making and keeping appointments.

We regularly remind them we are not going to do for them what they can do for themselves, but watching them trip and fall over simple things is hard to do.

So, we pick up pieces and start over, putting Humpty Dumpty back together again. You can see from these Facebook posts the level of anger and frustration that is counter-productive. It is being generated toward the very people who have the same problems or the people who can make a difference and are trying to help her.

Here are a few angry quotes from people on social media:

"I fucking hate it here."

This comment was made by a woman who was raised by angry parents. Her son is living with a teacher. She drives her vehicle without a license and refuses to register it to avoid having it towed. She even has a full-time job.

> "Who can take me to get my car obviously no one can tell me wtf they going to do and leave me hanging and not take me to my car when they say they going to man I fucking hate asking for favors all I got to say fuck you to all you fucking lops who ask me for favors do me a fucking favor you dumb fucks out there are wanting rides and favors is stay the fuck on out of ..."

This is more of her rant aimed at the very people trying to help her. She refuses to do her share of chores and likes to fight with other guests.

> "People wanna be fighting bitches half they age and get fucked up at the same time fucked up and sober bitch I'm coming back for you for talking about my son."

She has a bright son who is a gifted athlete. Children become what they learn. Hopefully, his stay with good people will break the cycle.

Whenever it's time to go home, there's always the temptation to feel we didn't do enough. Scolding a child is often wounding, so is admonishing an adult who believes nothing is ever their fault.

God help us.

Chapter Twenty-Seven

WHOSE JOB IS IT?

Because the general public has become numb to the scourge of homelessness, the lines seem blurred as to who is responsible for its resolution. Nonprofit organizations have changed the landscape by providing services of all kinds, from shelter to laundry and showers.

If the nonprofit world does a good job in the service area, which should really fall to the government, why are those services not funded by the government?

Sadly, nonprofits compete with each other for basic funding through grant applications. This is a tough job, particularly for nonprofits that do not have a budget for a grant writer. The task falls generally to a volunteer or a staff member with other duties. If the right boxes aren't checked or the documents are not in proper order, the application is subjected to the brutal action of disqualification, without grace or opportunity to correct.

Most will agree there is a general fear of homeless people living on the streets. If there is a safety issue, the natural role of government is to provide protection.

It is widely known the government has a crucial role in ensuring public safety. Its primary responsibility is to create and enforce laws and regulations to protect citizens from harm and to promote social order for all citizens and residents, whether documented or not, sheltered or not, mentally stable or otherwise. There is no exemption, but we know there have been many exceptions.

The government promotes public safety through law enforcement agencies. These agencies are responsible for preventing and investigating crimes, apprehending criminals and maintaining public order. Law enforcement agencies are the first responders to a complaint from the public or to a crisis.

The government also has a role in ensuring infrastructure and buildings are safe for public use. It sets standards for building codes, fire safety and public health regulations, as well as enforces these standards through inspections and licensing. They are particularly fussy about these elements in homeless shelters, its bathrooms, its commercial or warming kitchens, fire protection and security, including panic doors and emergency exits. Many agencies touch these elements—fire departments, building and safety departments, public health and environmental resources.

In addition, the government plays a significant role in emergency management and disaster response. It provides resources and support to communities affected by natural disasters, such as hurricanes, floods and wildfires, and it also prepares for and responds to other emergencies, such as terrorist attacks or pandemics.

Most will agree homelessness is an emergency and causes emergencies, evoking a response from police and fire agencies.

Overall, the government is the key to ensuring public safety, by creating and enforcing laws, providing law enforcement and emergency response services, and regulating various aspects of society to promote safety and security for all citizens. These services are covered by taxpayers, and so should the cost of housing and managing homeless people.

Most will agree the faces of homelessness have changed. No longer is the prevailing perception of a homeless person as an addict of some kind. They have morphed into the faces of senior citizens, children and working parents.

Also true are the changing and evolving reasons for homelessness, which are no longer limited to laziness, substance abuse and lifestyle choices. Clearly, economics have altered the landscape of housing. The pandemic caused people to lose jobs and face rising rents, which forced them out of familiar shelter.

The complex issue of homelessness raises questions about responsibility and the role of different entities in addressing this pervasive problem. With public indifference contributing to the blurred lines of responsibility, nonprofit organizations have stepped in to provide essential services that ideally should be government-funded. The predicament lies in the fact that these nonprofits often vie for limited resources through grant applications, straining their capacity to offer effective aid.

Despite the widespread fear and concern surrounding homelessness, it is the government that possesses the inherent duty to ensure public safety. This responsibility encompasses law enforcement, infrastructure safety, disaster response, as well as the enactment and enforcement of regulations that protect citizens from harm. The shifting face of homelessness—now encompassing seniors, children and employed individuals—underlines the evolving complexity of this issue, extending beyond preconceived notions of its causes.

Economic shifts and the recent pandemic have further intensified the urgency of addressing homelessness as a multi-faceted emergency that necessitates the government's involvement and taxpayer support. Ultimately, safeguarding the well-being of all citizens requires a collaborative effort that involves both public and private sectors working in tandem to alleviate the plight of homelessness and promote lasting change.

Fortunately, for the Santa Clara River Valley, the government has chosen to be a part of this complex problem and solution. There is now a three-way funding agreement between the cities of Santa Paula and Fillmore, matched by the County of Ventura, to keep Harvard Shelter open for two years. There is talk in Sacramento about mandating every city to provide some kind of shelter for homeless people. These two small cities can check that box in advance. Lucky us.

Part Three

Hope for the Future

MISSION MATTERS
WE AMPLIFY STORIES

Mr. Century City, LLC

Chapter Twenty-Eight

GRADUATING FROM HARVARD

Witnessing formerly homeless individuals rebuild their lives and secure a stable home is immensely rewarding.

The transformation from a place of vulnerability and uncertainty to one of empowerment and stability, brings a profound sense of fulfillment.

Observing their resilience, determination and growth as they navigate their journey toward self sufficiency evokes a mixture of pride, hope and genuine happiness.

I am especially moved by the journey of two people in particular: Sabriana and Nomi Marrufo. They are a powerful reminder of why I do this work.

One afternoon in the fall of 2018, my friend Veronica Sandez stopped by the office to let me know there were two young women at the corner of Davis and Santa Barbara Street, with their stuff spread all over the sidewalk and appeared to need help.

I went by to check on them and they assured me they were fine and did not need or want any help. They had sad faces, but that's not unusual in this line of work.

Sabriana and Nomi became homeless when the tenant in the house where they were renting a room told them they were being evicted. They roamed the streets with their four year old daughter for a month when a police officer finally stepped in. He told them, "You need to go see Kay."

What I didn't know then is these two would become like daughters to me, and become the leaders of SPIRIT of Santa Paula's staff. But it was a journey.

The Sabriana and Nomi Story

In the fall of 2018, Sabriana and Nomi were renting a room from someone who was renting a house. It's common in our area for renters to take in boarders and charge them $500 or $600 a month, and then not pay the landlord.

The dollar amount increased to $1,200 per room after the pandemic, which seemed to cause an egregious spike in rental rates. One night at 11 p.m., the renter of the house announced they had to be out of there by six in the morning, because the sheriff was coming to evict them.

Of course, they said, "What do you mean? We paid our rent. We have a five-year-old daughter. How can this happen?" She said, "I don't care, just be ready to be out of here at six." So, they packed up and behind one of their bicycles was a trailer with a stroller attached to it.

That's where they put Christine, their tiny five-year-old. They found themselves homeless and didn't know what they were going to do. During the day, they looked for work. At night, they rode around town on their bikes while Christine was sleeping.

Finally, the police pulled them over, and said, "You can't do this. We are going to be watching you." Then one night, a particularly harsh officer pulled them over, and said, "We're going to take this child. We will make sure Child Protective Services hides her and you will never see your daughter again." Sabriana and Nomi were hysterical as they watched little Christine cry as they put her into the police car and drove away. There was another officer there, who said, "You two need to go see Kay."

At that time, we had the winter shelter at the Methodist Church. Sabriana and Nomi came to see me the next day, and I put my arms around them and assured them we would work through this. "Christine will be okay. Just stick with me." They stayed at the shelter with their little black dog, named Brownie. I'm fostering Brownie for them now, because they can't have a dog where they live.

They soon became residents at Gabriel's House, where they were able to have Christine visit. Christine was in foster care for a year and a half. The family who had Christine didn't view their gay relationship favorably. Nomi played the role of the dad, and was very responsible and protective of the family. Sabriana was a good mother, the chatty one, and often spoke on behalf of the family.

They've known each other for a long time, since high school. Both of them had parents who were drug addicts. One night, when Nomi was working, her younger sister was hit by a car and killed. Nomi has suffered, thinking it should have been her who died. If she had been available, her sister would be.

Nomi and Sabriana never had drug experiences of their own, which is pretty amazing. They exemplify how two people saw the consequences of drugs, and said, "That's not for us." That is not common. It's typical for parents to pass this terrible habit onto their children.

Christine was with a lovely family in Santa Paula, who wanted to adopt her. That was not what Nomi and Sabriana wanted, so they appealed to the court. The judge, Tari Cody, was wonderful with them and saw their progress. Nomi had a job.

They were saving money and doing what they were supposed to do. Eventually, I hired them at SPIRIT. They were finally making enough money to get an apartment, when their housing voucher came through.

They were able to get Christine back on visits. After a long history of great effort—following every instruction, keeping every appointment and meeting every goal set before them by their social worker and the judge—the judge finally closed their case and they were reunited as a family. Family reunification is an uncommon result.

It shows the dedication of two people who will do whatever it takes to get their child back. Without drug or substance abuse in their lives, they were able to convince the court it was a good decision.

Christine, who was then six and a half, had been living a very comfortable life with this very nice family who resisted letting Christine stay with her parents on weekends. They were very protective. Christine got confused over who she belonged to. It was interesting to watch her re-calibrate as Nomi and Sabriana were able to take her home to live with them.

The story of foster children being reunited is interesting. In general, they really want to be with their natural parents. I was a child advocate for an 11-year-old girl who was living with a very affluent foster family. She had her own bedroom, a tennis court and a pool. She got into cheerleading. Her birth mom was living in a motel room and all the girl wanted to do was get back home to her mother. She was finally able to do that.

Foster parents have to prepare for a broken heart when they see so much opportunity they can give that the natural parent can't. But that's not what the child wants. They want their mother.

Christine went through a significant transition, trying to figure out her loyalty and affection, and where she was getting the love she needed. There was one time when Christine lashed out at her mother. She saw other mothers and children in the shelter, and said to Sabriana, "You gave me up. You let me go.

They have their mothers with them. You let me go." Sabriana was heartbroken, because she didn't know how to address that. We had to sit down and work through some therapy on why they had to let her go—for a little while.

They maintain a relationship with the foster family, because Christine found stability and love in their home, and maintaining that relationship was in her best interest.

*This was taken on December 6, 2019, just
a year after I first met them. They were the
keynote speakers at the shelter dedication
on that day. By then, they had their own
apartment, both had jobs and Christine
had been returned to them. Their CPS case
was eventually closed. They will always
be grateful to Christine's foster parents.*

Sabriana and Nomi are now top employees. I initially hired Sabriana
as shelter manager and Nomi became the facilities coordinator.
Today, they are flourishing. Sabriana is now the case manager
with great success at getting people ready for permanent housing,
because she knows all the doors that need to be opened and is
relentless in managing details.

Nomi has been promoted to general manager and looks after all operations. They purchased a new car, moved into a three-bedroom apartment, and took in Nomi's mother.

The gold in all of this is they did everything they were told to do to get their daughter back within a year and a half.

Today, they work on budgets, contribute to their savings account and their credit scores are in the 700s.

"Adult stuff," they say. Sabriana and Christine both have braces on their genetically troubled teeth. Christine is excelling in school, plays soccer and is very social. Her memories of those days are at the top of her emotional bank, however. We hope they become distant memories.

It's a great success story. It gives me the encouragement I need to keep on keeping on and seeing the good in people before looking at the bad. God had his hand on this family from the beginning, and sent good people to help them walk the narrow road to peace and prosperity.

They could've gone the other way, but neither of them wanted that for their lives. They have a bright future, because people believed in them, not because they simply wanted to, but because they saw their level of commitment to get it right.

Sabriana and Nomi are our best examples of why we do what we do. Their success also continues to define my own purpose and enables me to answer the calling I identified many years ago.

Nomi and Sabriana today in 2023.
Healthy, working, responsible, good parents of
Christine. They demonstrate the best of success
when people want to change their lives.

Chapter Twenty-Nine

LIGHTS IN THE DARKNESS

When good people choose to help and not ignore or cause harm, they make good things happen at Harvard Shelter. Judy Tan, a pharmacist at Rite Aid in Santa Paula, asked me if there was anything her group at Calvary Church in Ventura could do to help. I suggested they come one evening to serve dinner and do crafts with the kids. The visit was coordinated by Lisa Darling, a retired teacher from Santa Paula.

It was a great evening, and two of our visitors connected with two of our guests. While they were visiting, friendships were formed. Within a few days, one of the visitors rented her studio to Laura, our kitchen manager, and planned to help Laura with transportation to and from work, as well as school for the kids. While it seemed to be the perfect plan, we allowed it to go forward without a written contract and understanding from both parties. We now have a policy about overseeing agreements made between our guests and well-intentioned people. SPIRIT fronted the $2,000 deposit, and because Laura paid it in cash, there was no proof of payment. The judge ruled against Laura in the small claims action. Lesson learned. Case management continues.

A Realtor colleague, Laurie Ann Meyer, a member of Calvary Chapel in Ventura, found Maria and her three girls an apartment. With help and mentorship, Maria has risen to a high level of self-confidence and self-esteem. She now works at a dental office. There are new schools for the girls, and Maria now has her own car for transportation. We pray every day they get a good year out of that vehicle. Many used cars need many new things and are a terrible drain on household finances.

Successes Brighten Our World

Maria is now involved in church, taking care of her health and setting a wonderful example for her girls. While Maria's initial responses to discipline were unfavorable, over time our constant expressions of encouragement and love demonstrated our commitment to her success. Now, she lights up a room and is her own warm fire.

Both Laura and Maria received emergency housing vouchers, which allow them to pay one-third of their rent, while two-thirds are paid directly to the landlord through the housing authority. We will miss those girls. Children make everything better.

This is a stunning turn of events for these families. They are moving on to live the lives they were meant to live. This also opens up seven beds at Harvard Shelter for others. Success stories make our world so much brighter. Working in community makes magic happen.

Many of our helpers and visiting angels now know shelters are not scary places. They are home to families, seniors and people struggling to achieve what they dream of and know to be true.

Distractions and Entertainment

Liz and Bob Perez introduced the shelter guests to Tai Chi. They attend every Sunday night house meeting and volunteer to serve dinner on Friday nights. They are wise about how they develop friendships, keeping guard over their hearts and being clear about loving our guests into wholeness.

Rebecca Countryman is forming the Harvard Booster Club of Bright Lights. They provide activities for the kids during Sunday night house meetings, and activities for everyone during the week to engage their minds, apart from the television screen. She has been joined by Liz Lizarras, Jennifer Wambly and Liz Perez.

Rebecca Lizarraga is an attorney in Ventura, who has experience as a probation officer for a gang unit in L.A. She volunteers to provide creative outlets for the kids. I met her at a presentation I gave at the Center for Spiritual Living, in Ventura.

Vanessa White is a prominent business owner in Santa Paula and operates the fitness center. She comes to Harvard to host a dance and exercise class. Some refuse to join in and some are embarrassed, but they know the value of interacting with others and honoring a volunteer who takes time to provide entertainment and distractions.

Paul Belgum was great at making friends. He took special interest in men who lived at the river and made them feel important. Paul has a heart for the environment and spent many days helping clear the river beds of debris and trash. He was aided by Athens Trash Company, the County of Ventura, the City of Santa Paula and the Ventura County Conservancy. More than 700 cubic yards of trash were removed with labor provided by the men who live in the river area, supervised by Paul. Sadly, trash has built up again, despite all efforts to clear the area of inhabitants.

Christmas this past year 2022 was beyond anything we could have planned or imagined. Greg and Kelly Ray own a business nearby and asked if they could bring Christmas to Harvard. And they did. One Sunday before Christmas, they interviewed each guest, asking specific questions about what they wanted—and that is what they got. There were 16 children then, and the celebration of Christ's birth was beautiful.

Greg made arrangements for Santa Claus to make a grand entrance and deliver the gifts. Paul Belgum provided Christmas music and happy conversation. He is a retired teacher and has become a favorite mentor at Harvard.

The week of Christmas, Pastor Adelita Garza from the Bridge Church, brought a group to have fun with the kids. They played games, brought treats and sang songs. Few kids in our community could have experienced more love and sincere affection from strangers.

Many people drop off blankets, socks and hygiene items. Veronica Salazar is a realtor colleague in Ventura, and she held an all-girl sleepover at her home. Everyone (40 women) had to bring a gift bag of personal items. It was a bonanza and enough items were donated to keep everyone in beautiful lotions, shampoos, conditioners and skin care products. Such gifts are always a reminder that people do care.

Another realtor colleague, Anita Pulido, responded with a plea for funds to get a car smogged, registered and insured. It kept a family housed and working. There are hundreds of people who donate things we need to keep people standing. (See the section at the end of this book for a tribute to donors.)

The Rescue Mission provides Thanksgiving dinner and Latino Town Hall members adopt the shelter guests at Christmas. Members of the Presbyterian Church knit enormous Christmas stockings for everyone. Friends and colleagues are invaluable in the little things. We work in community, for the community. "Kinship," as Father Boyle would say.

Food Angels

We get to pick up unserved food from Starbucks, Pizza Chief and McDonald's. It helps our food budget stay near zero. Fortunately, our major food supplies come from county-wide grocery stores such as

Costco, Trader Joe's, Von's, Albertson's, Sprouts, Whole Foods and Panera. We service cruise-ship quality meals—about 175 of them a day—which includes shelter guests and those who come to the Drop In Center each morning.

Food Share is the county's amazing food bank under the leadership of Monica White, with her own unique passion for serving vulnerable people.

There are days when we think we are doing nothing more than caretaking adults who should be doing more to care for themselves. There are other days when we realize we are all they have and we are their future for now.

For those weary of doing good, here's a little story from the Quechua people of South America, who I met on a mission trip:

There was a massive fire in the forest, and all the animals felt overwhelmed and helpless. All except one little hummingbird. It flew to the nearby stream, picked up a few drops of water and dropped them on the fire. Then it flew down for more water, and back to the fire it went.

Meanwhile, other animals stood around watching. "What do you think you can do, hummingbird? You are so little, and the fire is so big. Your beak is too tiny and you can only bring a few drops of water at a time."

As it continued carrying these little drops of water to the fire, the hummingbird told them, "I'm doing the best I can."

184

SPIRIT of Santa Paula is committed to preventing and ending homelessness in the Santa Paula River Valley. We are also committed to serving the least powerful among us with food, services, encouraging words, direction, resources and compassion.

We are doing the best we can.

Chapter Thirty

THE NICK ARMAND STORY

Nick Armand is a musician. He has a sister who was backup singer for a famous vocalist.

Nick is 72 and his family lives in Santa Paula. He tosses around the names of famous centers of music like the Whiskey A-Go-Go and the Troubadour. He knows all the songs and their artists.

Nick's son was murdered in a gang killing several years ago in Los Angeles. This caused Nick to go through a mental crisis. He consequently fell into drug use and developed bipolar and schizophrenic symptoms.

Nick's wife had him leave their home, located in a very nice neighborhood in Santa Paula. He was on the streets when we became friends about 10 years ago. He was assaulted and lost his eyesight. This was very compromising, and he lost the ability to drive. I think there were people in town who had it out for Nick.

One night, he was in a Denny's parking lot. He walked over to the store to buy something, and when he returned, he discovered his car had been stolen. He always thought it was an inside job engineered by a disgruntled family member, and he spiraled downward.

He often stayed in Denison Park, a campground between Santa Paula and Ojai. He would call me when he was cold or hungry, and I'd drive around Denison camp at night, trying to find him. That was foolish in many ways, but my husband had died by then, and I had no one to worry about me.

Nick became dependent on me, mostly for a kind word. He spent time in Ojai on the streets and then in Ventura. Santa Paula Police officers were after him for vagrancy and dealing drugs. He was arrested a few times and had a probation officer who tried her best. He argued with his wife while in their car in another county and she obtained a restraining order against him. I went to court with him a few times in Ventura. His wife would try to be nice and invite him to house when he was hungry or cold. When an argument ensued, the police were called. Over and over. The judge in this case is my neighbor, who would see me in court with him. She respects the work we do, but she gave him no favors. She couldn't.

Nick was at Von's grocery store one day, rounding a corner, when a man moving a pallet jack of ice slammed into him. He fractured his foot, dislocated his shoulder, and broke several toes. There was a lawsuit with the potential of a settlement, but he needed two surgeries. He later fell and further injured his dislocated shoulder. They amputated a few of toes and told him they wouldn't do any more surgeries until he had a stable place to live. We convinced Nick to come to the shelter.

Nick had a substance abuse problem. One trait of an addict is they take things apart. They put everything in little piles, all spread out, and examine it. Then, they try to put it back together. Nick was doing that at the Harvard Shelter day and night. The same things and the same piles. That kind of behavior is a trigger for people with addictions. As they watch, their mind starts focusing on how much fun it is. I had to remove Nick from Harvard.

I talked to his attorneys and doctors, and we arranged for Nick to have the shoulder surgery he needed so he could function. After the

KAY WILSON-BOLTON

surgery, he came back to Harvard for a while and then left for a skilled nursing facility.

Thank God for his dedicated social worker, Amanda Sifuentes. She advocated for him to have his own apartment. There were several applicants, but he won. They called me on a Monday afternoon and said," Nick can move into his apartment today." We got him out of the hospital in Oxnard, brought him to the apartment, did the move-in inspection, signed the final papers and they gave Nick the keys. Fortunately, Nick's wife is still a part of his life. She has the passwords, helps with shopping and still provides assistance in various ways.

I have an ADU (Accessory Dwelling Unit) at my house that I had fully furnished for a woman who was in a shelter in Ventura. I was working with the United Way in a special landlord engagement program. She finally got her voucher to live in an apartment and I spent $2,000 furnishing the apartment. The day before she was going to move in, she changed her mind.

I lost a month and a half of rent, plus the cost of all the furnishings. So, I moved everything into storage. Little did I know then how useful it would be. Within two hours of Nick getting his apartment, I corralled two guys from Harvard to load up the furniture from storage. Nick got to sleep in his own bed that night. It was a miracle story.

You can't give up on people. There were times when I was ready to do that with Nick. He was head strong, argumentative and could not stop talking.

He's in such a great place now. We talk to him regularly and he goes to the Presbyterian Church on Sundays and attends choir practice on Mondays. He attempts the Tuesday night recovery group at Catalyst Church. His wife visits him and takes him food. He does his own laundry

188

in his own beautiful apartment. His family is communicating with him again and sees him living a normal life.

His friend, Paul Belgum, a retired teacher in Santa Paula, pays him regular visits and they play guitar together. Nick is now giving guitar lessons to some young ones. Nick feels useful, healthy and happy—and he is in his own home.

This is why you can't give up.

He told his own story in our podcast "Bruised Reeds—Santa Paula." You can find it on that YouTube channel. This is the end to a nightmare for a 72 year old musician. He will be able to live in that lovely apartment the rest of his life, as long as he doesn't screw up. And, as long as his old friends don't visit him.

When our people get permanent housing, they often invite their friends in who create problems. It doesn't take long before they're out on the streets themselves again. They feel sorry for each other, especially when it's raining and cold.

And, oddly enough, that's how we got started. The janitor of a local church was inviting homeless people into the building at night, until one of them died—right there. Rudy got fired and left the church. Because he believed he was his brothers' keeper, Rudy became the inspiration for a homeless shelter in Santa Paula.

Chapter Thirty-One

MIRACLE ON HARVARD BOULEVARD

At the beginning of 2023, I felt desperation creeping in to obtain stable funding. I reached out to the city manager in Fillmore, David Rowlands, asking him and his city council members to consider funding Harvard Shelter. I attended a city council meeting and took two representatives with me, who had been homeless in Fillmore. One was a senior citizen and successful business person named Daisy Rodriguez, and another was an 18-year-old named Vannity, who had been involved in a Fillmore youth group when she was 12 years old, but became homeless when her mother suffered health and personal challenges.

I presented a case for supporting Harvard Shelter, and to my surprise, the vote was unanimous to do so. They provided $150,000 that fiscal year, which came from AARPA, funds from the federal government, designed to help America rebuild after the pandemic.

In March 2023, SPIRIT of Santa Paula lost its volunteer grant writer. I picked up the responsibility and managed to win a Community Development Block Grant for $93,000. However, it was not available until the next fiscal year 2023–2024, possibly not until September or November, which was six to eight months away.

My next attempt at grant writing for $250,000 resulted in a failure, because of a mistake I made in combining funding for Harvard Shelter with a request for funding a case manager. The donors felt they should've been on two separate grants, so it was disqualified.

I told the grantors that SPIRIT of Santa Paula would not survive this failure and neither would I. Little did I know how right I was. The Board of Directors were made aware of the looming crisis beginning in March 2023, and I continued to stress the urgency of alternatives. In April, I announced to the "world" that Harvard would close on June 1, if we did not have emergency funding. The Ventura Star picked up the story and a thoughtful reporter, named Tony Biasotti, met me for an interview and it was front page news throughout the county.

Santa Paula Mayor Andy Sobel suggested I reach out to Lance Oroszco from NPR radio, 88.3 FM. Lance came to Harvard Shelter for an interview with myself and staff members. Those two events were life-changers. Assemblymember Steve Bennett, who had been a popular long-term County Supervisor in Ventura County, called and suggested we confer on resolving the issue.

In late May, Supervisor Kelly Long scheduled a meeting for me with county officials to talk about funding the shelter. In 2018, the Board of Supervisors passed a resolution that local funds earmarked for shelter would be matched 50-50 by the county. It was suggested we initiate that process. Attending were staff members from the City of Santa Paula, overworked and underpaid, and while everyone agreed it was the proper next step, no action resulted.

As soon as Assemblymember Bennett became engaged, conversations began between city managers and all 10 council members from the two cities of Santa Paula and Fillmore. There were many discussions with county staff and cities' staffs to create a memorandum of agreement for funding SPIRIT for $670,000 over two years. The funding also provided for the hiring of an executive director, to fill the spot I am filling for free, another case manager to handle the load and a grant writer to secure additional funding.

There was initial hesitation and caution, because this had not been done before, and two years felt like a long commitment. At various meetings, I focused on the fact that without a two-year runway of stable funding, it would be impossible to hire qualified personnel who would feel secure in taking these positions.

The Santa Paula City Council held their special meeting on July 14, and the Fillmore City Council on August 8. The votes were unanimous to support the funding mechanism.

It is appropriate to note here that without the leadership of Santa Paula City Manager Dan Singer, this agreement would not have materialized. Previous city managers despised me and the work being done to provide services to homeless people and would never have supported the task of creating a partnership with SPIRIT of Santa Paula.

Over the years, I have been called on the carpet by magistrates and business owners, accusing me of causing homelessness and attracting homeless people by the hundreds into Santa Paula due to our services. Personal friends moved away from me.

Former mayor and current councilmember, Jenny Crosswhite, aptly noted at one council meeting this agreement would not have happened years ago ... and she was right. The Santa Paula City Attorney Monica Castillo assisted in crafting the memorandum of agreement between SPIRIT and the City of Santa Paula. She worked with Assemblymember Bennett to perfect it. Tiffany Israel, Fillmore City Attorney, worked with City Manager David Rowlands to prepare the agreement for funding.

None of this was any small effort. In my darkest moments, I never dreamed the outcome would be like this. Assemblymember Bennett spent all day Father's Day 2023 crafting the agreement and working with me throughout the day.

Major achievements come from inspiration and dedication. My sweet husband, Howard Bolton, once said, "A happy heart is a magnet for miracles." For me, I struggled finding a happy heart, but there is no doubt there were many miracles over the years.

The first ever gala celebration for SPIRIT of Santa Paula is scheduled for Oct. 27, 2023. I told the board of directors we needed to have at least one event before I have to arrive in a wheelchair and can't remember what I want to say. It's unusual that an organization like ours would not have at least one annual fundraising event in 21 years, but frankly, I believed no one would come. As it turned out, hardly anyone did so we canceled the event. I think people don't expect us to entertain them.

We chose to have the gala at a church—Encounter in Ventura. Our best work has been done in churches—and it was in a church where we found our inspiration and purpose when we discovered Richard Rios Soto had died on a cold night inside.

It was in churches where we had our first winter shelters: Iglesia de Dios 7mo Dia en Santa Paula, at 113 South Mill Street; El Buen Pastor Methodist Church, at 1029 E. Santa Paula Street; and the First United Methodist Church, at 117 No. Mill Street. Many Meals was first at the same church as the first shelter, and in 2010, it moved to the First Presbyterian Church, at 121 Davis Street, where an estimated 400,000 meals were served each Wednesday over an 11-year period.

For 21 years, our work has been done quietly with little fanfare, in order to not draw attention that might result in criticism. It seems it took a crisis in homelessness to have people appreciate our work and realize good outcomes are possible.

If the government pays to shelter stray dogs and cats, it should pay to shelter the strays of humanity. After all, we are our brother's keeper. Aren't we?

Chapter Thirty-Two

THE POWER OF PARTNERSHIPS

Since our incorporation in 2003, SPIRIT's mission is to end and prevent homelessness, to discover those people who are homeless, bring light to the subject of homelessness, and connect our homeless neighbors to a community of caring people and the services that will change their lives.

The odd thing is the more we do, the more people need our services. We cannot solve the homeless crisis or the problems of homeless people without partners—trusted partners. We were shy at first about involving others, because there was so much animosity toward homeless people and us. We had many more foes than friends at that time.

Our early job was to convince the community the homeless people we served were people connected to Santa Paula, our own people.

Soon, our friends and partners became formidable and powerful ... and effective.

It began with an increased assessment of needs. We learned about the essential nature of good food and reliable supplies. We discovered the need for showers and clean clothes. To that end, we modeled the Bridge Church in Ventura that started a program called Laundry Love. We started A Little Laundry to adapt the program to Santa Paula's needs.

Retired attorney Carolyn Tulberg called one day and asked if there is something she could do. She was perfect for Laundry Love. Years ago, clients and friends Dave and Donna Stewart purchased a vacant lot on East Main Street. I suggested the greatest need was for a laundromat. They built a beautiful facility. We asked if they would be okay with us directing traffic at an off hour and paying for people's wash and dry. That program lasted for five years—partly because there were abuses of the program and Carolyn turned 90. Her kids insisted she take a break.

Our range of services grew in our efforts to prevent and end homelessness. If we can prevent a family from losing their housing or having their utilities turned off, we make life easier and keep them sheltered. It's easier to keep them sheltered than try to do a rapid re-entry. If they lose their housing, their credit is spoiled and they lack money for deposits. It's especially bad if they get evicted. Hardly anyone will take a chance on them.

Our goals each day are to work with our homeless neighbors through Ventura County's Pathways to Home program and our Federal Housing and Urban Development's (HUD) Homeless Management Information System (HMIS) to research housing and benefit availability.

As of October 1, 2023, SPIRIT had 17 employees, a data manager and bookkeeper, many volunteers, a full-time unpaid director and a 12-member board of directors. As of this writing, December 3, 2023, we have a full-time paid executive director and our data manager, Mary Ruiz, is now the executive assistant.

As of this writing, December 4, 2023, our staff includes: Brent Reisender, Mary Ruiz, Nomi Marrufo, Melinda Palm, Leana Nickerson Ramirez, Art Marcelo, Kim Rangel, Sabriana Marrufo, Jessica Lucas, Maria Aguirre, Cassandra Teofilo, John Garcia, Pepe Gonzalez, Laura Interiano, Maria Sanchez, Ted Rangel, Enoch Aparico, Melissa Patterson, Cynthia Vergera, and Catherine Malone.

***

SPIRIT's Programs Include:

1. **Harvard Year-Round Emergency Homeless Shelter:** As of March 31, 2020, Spirit of Santa Paula took a huge leap of faith to create a 24/7/365 year-round Homeless Shelter for our homeless (maximum 49 people), including very low-income, elderly, victims of domestic violence and human trafficking. We provide a warm, safe, welcoming facility, a bed, three nourishing meals daily, showers, laundry and counseling to find housing and employment. We provide two isolation pods to prepare people for safe entry to the shelter, plus all the COVID-19 protocols necessary to protect all our people, including recommending families and disabled to county supplied room-key facilities. Isolation pods and shower pods were donated by one of our directors, Vern Alstot, and his partner, George Magana. All our services are free of cost.

2. **HMIS (Homeless Management Information System):** Our HMIS Program in Santa Paula allows for unduplicated client entry and research for possible housing/services availability, searches for available emergency shelters, healthcare, and Ventura County Behavioral Healthcare.

3. **Food Rescue:** Through our state's CalRecycle program, our county's VC Waste Free Program and Food Share, Spirit rescued 173,064 pounds of commercially prepared, un-served food and received 805,487 pounds from Food Share to distribute to 4,500 to 5,000 unduplicated people per month, in Santa Clara River Valley, through our two weekly food pantries, our year-round

emergency homeless shelter and our resource center. These groceries allow our people to allocate more of their funds to rent and other necessities, thus retaining their housing, utilities, transportation, as well as their personal dignity and family stability. It also allows SPIRIT to have a zero food budget for Harvard Shelter.

4. **One Stop Whole Person Care Shower Pod Program:** We collaborate with Ventura County Health Care Agency, Whole Person Care and Behavioral Health to provide a weekly event, hosted by El Buen United Methodist Church, providing weekly showers, counseling, healthcare and meals for our street people at no cost.

5. **Drop In Center for Our Street People:** This service is provided at the Harvard site, and we offer meals to go, sanitary facilities and counseling for our unsheltered homeless who choose not to shelter with us. There is no cost to our clients and guests. During the COVID-19 pandemic, the Presbytery of Santa Barbara provided funds for a handicap Porta Potty for use by the street people. It is still in use.

6. **Laundry for our Homeless:** We meet our unsheltered homeless who want to participate in this program at a local laundromat at a set-aside time to pay for their wash and dry.

7. **Many Meals for our Community:** This program went on hold due to the COVID-19 pandemic as of March 2020, when we served an average of 600 meals every Wednesday night for dine-in or take-out, located at First Presbyterian Church, 121 Davis St., downtown Santa Paula. It is open to all who need a hot, nutritious meal at no cost, a food pantry, and an opportunity to meet our community and our counselors.

8. **Police and Fire Departments:** We rely on first responders to protect us and help us protect others. Our assigned officers have been Donavan Varela and Dan Gosselin. Dan McCarthy has also provided oversight and excellent leadership. They demonstrate compassion and fairness. Like everyone, we bring our biases into the workplace and not all experiences have been favorable.

9. **Santa Paula Housing Authority:** There is new leadership at this organization. Elenore Vaughn brought incredible skills from her work at the Los Angeles Area Housing Authority. "No" is not in her vocabulary. She makes things work to benefit people. We created an MOU between the Santa Paula Housing Authority and SPIRIT of Santa Paula to deploy sustainable housing vouchers for families at Harvard Shelter. Currently, there is a many years-long wait list for a voucher. She is making it happen today.

10. **Food Share:** Last, but never the least, is Food Share, Ventura County's Food Bank. It is led by CEO Monica White, who has become a great friend and great partner. She makes our pantries and food connections possible. Her staff of Pamela Castro and Annabelle Herrera take good care of us.

***

We don't want to do this work alone. SPIRIT now enjoys amazing support from our communities. We work together with city staff, police department, sheriff's department and fire department personnel concerning policy and emergency needs. Our volunteers are generous with their time, and find personal satisfaction by helping our clients and our programs with grant writing and administration.

Ventura County Fire Dispatcher Wendy White taught us how to make good 911 calls. Ventura County Fire Department Engineer Manny Morales gave lessons on CPR and certified all staff members. Melissa Gerwe provided training on the uses of NARCAN and we are now a distribution site.

Before SPIRIT's homeless services began in 2008, some of these needs were being addressed by a few of our city's churches. As SPIRIT grew, we added services, particularly with the help of the City of Santa Paula, the County of Ventura, and United Way EFSP, under the guidance of Susan England. Private foundations and donors kept us going and growing.

The Annual Homeless Count

Each year in January, we organize and implement the county's mandated homeless count. It's never accurate, but it is an indicator of who is living on the street. We count at the shelter, food pantries, One Stop, laundry site, Drop In Center, parks, riverbeds, bus stops, the post office and neighborhood markets. Our point in time count rose only by six people in the 2023 count, but we know there are more. Volunteers arrive at 6 a.m. and spread out through town. We use a mobile app and the effort is managed by the County's Continuum of Care.

Population Being Served:

- Our current people served—homeless and those at risk of homelessness—are over 80 percent Hispanic surnames.

- Our two weekly food pantries serve 4,500 to 5,000 individuals per month.

- Our year-round emergency homeless shelter houses a maximum of 49 guests. Numbers vary as guests leave and new guests come in.

- Many Meals served an average of 600 per week. (The program was suspended due to the COVID-19 pandemic.)

- We rescue 171,000 pounds of food each month for distribution and use at Harvard Shelter.

- One Stop Showers and Whole Person Care serve 55 unduplicated unsheltered homeless per month.

- Our resource homeless center serves approximately 60 unduplicated people per month.

- Utility and rental assistance averages $3,000 per month.

- Special needs: auto repair, gasoline, prescription co-pay, car registration, etc., averages $400 per month.

In Ventura County, most everyone knows SPIRIT of Santa Paula is the place to see, a place to go and/or where to send others in need. Each day, we see people who have been living in the shadows come out for assistance. They hear from others that SPIRIT will help.

Something To Consider

Statistically, homelessness across the U.S. is dramatically increasing each year. We see some of our clients being housed, but we also see more losing their housing. The most brutal reason is the severe lack of affordable housing and rising rents. Increased rents make the value of residential income more attractive, but it is causing homelessness. Affordable housing is a more long-range challenge, but one we are taking on. We search each day for short-term solutions to keep people healthy and off the streets. We work with state, county, city and community organizations, advocating the construction of low and very low-income housing. This is still not a popular topic with many who are housed and have theirs.

Chapter Thirty-Three

WHAT MATTERS MOST

While you can find people in any neighborhood with emotional, financial and personal problems, every person in Harvard Shelter is shattered in some way. This book is about the human conditions of decline and hope, dreams and dashed expectations, childhood trauma, disappointments, and resolutions to overcome trips and falls.

The primary focus of shelter operators has to be kindness. Our guests come to us hungry and dirty, angry and sad, lost and lonely. You have met some of them in this book. We have to provide the antithesis of each of these problems. We do very well most of the time.

Our words are guided by trauma-informed care. Our mantra is "Choose your words so you are not re-traumatizing someone."

We cater equally and accommodate special conditions, from the safe storage of insulin to accommodating wheelchairs, walkers, laundry services and showers. The food supply is endless and generous. Our rules are to provide order, not to limit privileges. We have a mandatory family meeting on Sunday nights and a report from the house council, citing what is good about Harvard, what can be improved, and if there are any problems.

Case management is essential. We won't do for them what they can learn how to do for themselves, but we get them ready to try and take charge of their lives. We have many success stories and have made friends for life.

Some people left Harvard, due to the structure, and some were asked to leave for failure and unwillingness to comply. You can't keep people safe when bullies want to overthrow the managers.

My final words are these: Think kindly and speak softly to people who are suffering and living their lives differently from you. Support those who can solve the problem, by praying for them/us, and give of your time and talents. If you don't want to do any of that, please let those of us who do out of your conversations.

When you are tempted to judge harshly and compare their failures to your success, take stock in what led to your success. Give credit to the simple fact you weren't born in a village in Tibet or the slums of Calcutta. Be grateful you learned early how to make good decisions. Be grateful you either overcame or never experienced substance abuse problems, lost a job or lost a partner who was the primary financial resource for the family and good health.

Just be grateful.

If you want to help those who help, you can donate in the following ways:

Zelle:
kay@spiritsp.org
https://spiritofsantapaula.org

Mail check or money order to:
SPIRIT of Santa Paula
P.O. Box 949
Santa Paula, CA 93061-0949

SPIRIT of Santa Paula is a 501C3,
EIN 27-0005506
Platinum Status GuideStar (Candid)
Successful audits

EPILOGUE: THEIR NAMES

Honoring the names of the homeless who have tragically passed away is not only an act of compassion, but also a crucial step toward recognizing their humanity and dignity. These individuals often endure profound hardships and isolation during their lives, facing homelessness due to a myriad of complex circumstances. Speaking their names at a vigil is a poignant gesture, which reminds society that every life, regardless of social status or circumstance, holds inherent value. It acknowledges their existence and provides a moment of remembrance, countering the invisibility and stigma that often shroud the homeless population.

These vigils also raise awareness about the urgent need for solutions to homelessness and underscores the collective responsibility we all share in ensuring that every individual, regardless of their housing situation, is treated with respect and empathy. In doing so, we not only honor the homeless who have died, but we also commit to creating a more compassionate and just society for those still struggling on the margins.

***

The following is an important writing by Peter Robinson, a Ventura County advocate for people experiencing homelessness. Peter is often "out there" when it comes to strategic thinking, but he has the invaluable personal lived experience that translates to new ways of thinking about people, places and the times. His comments deserve a place in this book.

Homeless Vigil Remarks by Peter Robinson, Ventura, December 2022

Every month, a publication in Orange County, called Voice of OC, publishes the names of the people who died homeless in the county during the preceding 30 days. This accomplishes many things, especially keeping the issue front and center. Father Dennis Kriz collects the names from the coroner, writes some commentary, and hands it off to the Voice of OC, who publishes it. Simple, right?

It celebrates the lives of these human beings by making them important enough to be named, remembered and mourned. Here, in Ventura County, we do quite the opposite. We hide the names of the dead and ignore our horrific homeless death rate. We have folks on social media who accuse other places of "bussing in" their homeless, because we won't take ownership of our own.

Even though our rate of homelessness is in line with the rest of California, and considerably lower than nearby counties like Santa Barbara, these folks continue to push forward this ridiculous idea, because it relieves them of responsibility.

In the past, there was always one event where a dead homeless person could be recognized, celebrated and grieved. Many cities around the nation hold EOY vigils for the homeless, where folks share memories of loved ones. In all of these vigils, the names of the dead are read, and a bell is rung in their memory. Everywhere, that is, except Ventura County.

In what has to be the most "Ventura County" thing ever, this year we were only allowed to read the first names and last initials of the deceased, ensuring that they were treated in death as they were in life—with disdain and disrespect. Seems a family with some pull didn't want to cop to having a dead homeless kid, so they found a shyster and there you go. That's a rumor that might be true, but whatever the reason, it's cowardly and disgusting.

* * *

Peter spoke again at the Oxnard Homeless Vigil the following night, in December 2022. Here are his remarks:

I am honored to stand among these healers to remember our friends and family who have passed. There is no experience quite like that of being homeless. Dragging around a rolling suitcase in America will teach you things about the world and people you could never learn any other way. You'll learn that the parameters of human behavior are much wider than you thought. And when you make it out, you're thankful for what you've learned ... which is not the same as wanting to do it again.

Who are the homeless? Teachers, administrators and managers. Dentists, lawyers, politicians. Entrepreneurs and dreamers. Architects, realtors, brainiacs. Those are just some of the people I've met in shelters and on the street. And these aren't "former" anything—these are just lives paused by circumstances.

How does one become homeless? Lack of affordable housing. Low wages. Job loss. All economic factors. Those places with the least affordable housing have the highest homeless rates. Drug abuse and mental illness are down the list aways. Drug abuse occurs at the junction of boredom and hopelessness, just as it does for the housed. And mental illness ... if you think you're depressed now, try walking around where people hate you on sight.

For women, along with the above factors, it's domestic violence and the loss of a child that can finally push them outdoors. I was over two and a half years homeless. I slept both on the ground and in the shelters of Las Vegas. I spent time underneath the city of Vegas, and in a house of human trafficking. I've slept on the beach in Oxnard, P.H., and Ventura. I've slept in parks around the county, on cardboard in alleys, and under some of the finest bridges in all of Ventura County.

I sought help and got help from Mercy House in Oxnard and the Arch in Ventura. The Turning Point Foundation. Catholic Charities and the Rescue Mission Alliance, both here and in Vegas. Community Action. One Stop. Section 8 housing. Many Meals. Emilio Ramirez. Kay of Santa Paula, and Luther of Ventura.

Eventually, I was able to become housed again, and I know many others who have also made it all the way out. But it isn't easy, and it has little to do with desire or sticktoitiveness. It was a combination of these helping entities and others, along with a little luck. The voucher system is deeply flawed, with countless recipients unable to find a place after waiting years to get a voucher. Imagine the hopelessness after that experience.

We've learned and established that low-barrier shelter concepts and the housing first concepts are the most effective at recovering and preserving the lives of the unhoused. The continuation of programs like Project Roomkey is essential, whether we get funding from the governor or we do it ourselves.

We know that the homeless census is likely to rise in the next year, and we want our death count to fall. In order to bring the number of deaths down next year, we'll need to open more shelters and resource facilities. Thousand Oaks just made a powerful move in this direction, and Ventura can do the same. And Oxnard will need another shelter, either in partnership with or alongside Mercy House.

How do the homeless die? Lack of services is a huge deal. Due to the topography of our county, many of our unhoused are in remote areas. So, opening more shelters makes sense, because a shelter offers all those missing services. The first thing that Oxnard could do to be part of the solution is to open the services they already have. Unlock those public restrooms or be judged.

A new council is coming on board—we'll find out right quick if they have any human compassion within them. And there is another way our homeless and others die. We have a new kind of drug dealer. This guy isn't trying to hook you and bleed you of money and life over the next few years, like in the old days. This guy wants to murder you with a hotshot. He wants to sell you something that has fentanyl snuck into it. Riverside County has an elegant solution and other counties are looking into it: If you kill someone with a hotshot, you're going in for murder.

So, we'd have two signs at bus stops: 1) be careful of hotshots, and 2) kill someone with a hotshot, you're going in for all day. Counties that do this will drive these murderers toward the counties that don't. There are no ordinary homeless people, because there are no ordinary people.

Every human being is extraordinary and unique, capable of great and terrible things. Each of these 158 men and women we honor here today, and all those who have passed, but are not counted here today, had success in their lives. They had people who loved them, and people they loved. They had dreams and ambitions. They were sweet and lovable and flawed, like all of us are. When you see someone suffering, tell them you love them. Tell them God loves them. Tell them that strangers love them, because we know that it's true.

When you see someone suffering in a way that might spill over onto others, tell them Jesus loves them. Hold them and act as a conduit, and ask God to look down and help His child. All of us have been given this ability to assist in the healing of our brothers and sisters. The Kingdom of God is within us. The Kingdom of Heaven is at hand. God bless everyone for being here, God bless the homeless, and God bless Ventura County.

In Memory of Those Who Didn't Make It. We know there are more.

Some dates are estimated.

Todd Coates—November, 2022

Steve Meyer—2022

Adan Tadeo—5-3-22

Leo Zepeda—3-11-21

Noe Zepeda—6-4-21

Novak Vukotik—2-14-2021

Lissa Marie Mata—12-13-2021

Sherry Vaughn—2019

Luis Rodriguez—November, 2021

Michelle Diaz—2022

Charles Galarza—2022

Guadalupe Cervantes—Hospital

Ronnie Hurtado—Motel

Cynthia Villarreal—Hospital

Sergio Roberto Yanez—River, 3-29-19

Daniel Price—River, 2018

Gilbert Marquez—April, 2018

Louie Rodriquez—Three days after leaving Harvard

Timmy Hurtado—2018

Richard "Dicky" Flores

Carol Lofton—Hospital, January, 2018

Ron Kaehlen—His truck, March, 2018

Terry Patino—2018

Ed Karpinski—May, 2017

Antonio Fuentes—Burned on a park bench, 2017

Henry "Hank" Garcia—His little dog Cleo is safe

Victor Sanchez—May, 2017

Cindy Villareal—2021

Camerino—2017

Lee Nevarez—2017

Shirley Bustillos—2016

Stella Ortiz—Halloween, 2015

Martin "Guanajuato" Vasquez—2016

James in the wheelchair—2017

Carol Lofton—1-12-18

Eddy Newman—1-26-18

Terri Patino—1-12-18

Charles Cutshaw—April 18, 2014

John Jeffrey—2010

Maria Soto—2022

Daniel Price

Noe Zepeda 2022

Maria Soto—8-9-2021

Manuel "Peanut" Andres—2022

Leo Zepeda—2022

Michelle Diaz—November, 2021

Toby Raymond Navarez

Sandra Monji

Frank Hernandez—2023

Nick Garcia—July, 2023

Eric Sonerson

Dana Sonerson

Miguel Angel Ortiz

We know there were others.

OUR MAJOR DONORS

I say a silent thank you every time someone gives something to keep our shelter open and our food trucks on the road. Every dollar makes a difference.

A special thanks to the donors who gave in abundance at critical times.

Acknowledging our major donors—$5,000 or more:

- Naomi Pitcairn

- Bank of the Sierra

- Gene Hass Foundation

- Anonymous donor in memory of George and Barbara Wilson—$75,000

- Priscilla Sanders Giberson

- Ellen Brokaw

- John and Susan Kulwiec

- Local 805 Carpenters Union

- Kay Wilson-Bolton

- David and Tracy Lippert

- Martin and Mary Lou Zuanich

- JH Douglas & Associates

- Howard Bolton

- Supervalue Foundation

- National Association of Realtors

- Limoneira Foundation

- Greg and Kelly Ray

- CarePodz - George Magana and Vern Alstot

- FM Pearce

- Andy's Plumbing

- Ventura County Commerce, Inc.

- Puente de Vida Church

- Juliana Zarate

- Merewether Family

- Steve and Kathy Goch

- B3W, Inc.

- Dan Goodwin

ABOUT THE AUTHOR

Kay Wilson-Bolton was born in Rochester, New Hampshire, on Feb. 15, 1947, in full baby-boomer fashion. She was due in December 1946, but a snowstorm hit the area and no roads to the hospital were open. Her father was Maurice C. Giberson, and he worked in the woolen mills.

He was laid off just before Christmas, so there was no money for the hospital. Mom told Kay to wait a while, until the roads cleared and her father got his first paycheck. That occurred on Feb. 14, 1947, and that was the day they went to the hospital. The family was known as the "Gibersons on the Old Dover Road." They lived in an old brick school house converted to a home for a large family.

Her mother was Marion Day Giberson. In birth order were siblings Mary Beatrice, David Chipman, Eric Joseph, Jon Allen, two miscarriages, Kay Frances and Sara Ann.

The family moved to California in the summer of 1955. Someone determined Kay should skip the third grade and go from second grade to fourth. They rented a two bedroom house in Calimesa and the boys slept in the garage. In 1957, the family moved to Yucaipa, after purchasing a home for $12,000.

Kay graduated from Yucaipa High School in 1964, and then attended San Bernardino Valley College. She then transferred to Northridge State University in 1966, then onto Cal Poly Pomona, where she graduated in 1968, with a Bachelor of Science degree in Business Administration. She worked as a marketing assistant for Sunkist Growers, and then for Superior Farming Company in Bakersfield.

In 1976, she married Dale Wilson and they moved to Santa Barbara. Shortly after, they purchased the small real estate company in Santa Paula, from Floyd Hair. In 1988, Kay and Dale divorced. Two years later, when she was the Mayor of Santa Paula, she married graphic artist Howard Bolton. He had just been selected as Santa Paula's Citizen of the Year. They were married 33 years, until Howard died Aug. 15, 2021. It was a local love story.

Kay graduated from the Masters University with a Bachelor of Arts degree in Biblical Counseling, in 2015, and began course work for the

Master's Degree. She took a leave of absence when Howard became ill, and was not allowed to finish, because she was an ordained Elder in the Presbyterian Church, which is against the creed of the University.

Kay was the second State President of the California Women for Agriculture, which began in 1976. They organized a statewide coalition before fax machines, cellphones and voicemail. They initiated the Worm Watcher to record how elected officials were voting on related issues. The women were told to go home and let them handle it. They didn't.

Kay received the Firefighter of the Year Award, from the Santa Paula Fire Department in 2010, for her work as department Chaplain; the Champion of Homes Award, from the California Association of Realtors, in 2015, for her work with people experiencing homelessness; and the Good Neighbor Award, from the National Association of Realtors, in 2017, for making a difference in her community.

She was named Woman of the Year in Ventura County in 2011 by the California State Assembly.

She plays in the handbell choir at the First Presbyterian Church and is the Lead Chaplain for Ventura County Fire Department.

She is the President of Ventura County Commerce, Inc., in which she is broker for Buena Vista Property Management. She is a full-time real estate broker with Century 21 Everest, a part of Century 21 Alliance.

She served on many boards and commissions, including Ventura County Behavioral Health, and president of both the Ojai Valley Board of Realtors and the Ventura County Coastal Association of Realtors. She served three times as the Board President for the Boys and Girls Club of the Santa Clara Valley, and president of the Santa Paula Chamber of Commerce.

She is an author participant in two other books on the topics of seeing a different rate of return using philanthropy and the value of affordable housing so people can work close to home.

Kay lives quietly in Santa Paula, California, with several rescued pups. However, there is still much to be done.

Her life verse is: Ps. 138: 7-8:

The Lord will complete what is His purpose is for me.
Lord, your gracious love is eternal.
Do not abandon your personal work in me.

www.ingramcontent.com/pod-product-compliance
Lightning Source LLC
Chambersburg PA
CBHW060841280326
41934CB00007B/878